DRAWINGS BY
HOLBEIN
FROM THE COURT OF HENRY VIII

AN UNIDENTIFIED GENTLEMAN (No. 17; detail)

DRAWINGS BY
HOLBEIN
FROM THE COURT OF HENRY VIII

*Fifty Drawings from the Collection of
Her Majesty The Queen, Windsor Castle*

CATALOGUE BY JANE ROBERTS

ART GALLERY OF ONTARIO, TORONTO
28 OCTOBER 1988 — 15 JANUARY 1989

JOHNSON REPRINT CORPORATION

HARCOURT BRACE JOVANOVICH, PUBLISHERS

Designed by Meyer Miller

Printed in England

Library of Congress Catalogue Number: 86-083033

ISBN 0-384-23843-2

Front cover illustration: JOHN MORE THE YOUNGER (No. 4)

First edition

A   B   C   D   E

Contents

Foreword

Hans Holbein the Younger is one of those rare artists whose works have influenced the way we perceive an entire historical age. Just as we see the glittering court of Charles I through the eyes of Sir Anthony van Dyck, it is Holbein's genius that gives us access to the galaxy of fascinating characters who surrounded Henry VIII. These were troubled times in England, and the present exhibition provides us with an unforgettable record of the men and women who were determining the future course of English history. Such luminaries as Thomas More and William Warham have been immortalized with extraordinary vividness, the result of Holbein's uncommon ability to combine direct observation and superb draughtmanship with the most sensitive psychological insights.

We are deeply indebted to Her Majesty Queen Elizabeth II for her generosity in sharing with us the Holbein treasures.

Our gratitude also extends to the talented staff of the Royal Library, Windsor Castle, who organized, planned, and prepared this exhibition, particularly Oliver Everett, Librarian, Jane Roberts, Curator of the Print Room, Henrietta Ryan, Deputy Curator, Theresa-Mary Morton and Julia Baxter, Assistant Curators—Exhibitions.

The exhibition has been generously sponsored by Chubb Insurance Company of Canada. It would never have been possible without special assistance from the Government of Canada through the insurance program for travelling exhibitions. Dr. Katharine Lochnan, Curator of Prints and Drawings and Dr. Francis Broun, Lecturer in Adult Programmes, were instrumental in organizing and installing the exhibition.

To everyone involved, we extend our sincere thanks. Whenever a museum is fortunate enough to present extraordinary works, the entire community is elevated. Hans Holbein provides the clear eye and flawless touch that helps us all to see and understand.

WILLIAM WITHROW
Director, Art Gallery of Ontario, Toronto

Chubb Insurance Company of Canada is honoured to sponsor this exhibition of Holbein's work.

It's not the first time the artist has been sponsored; on his first trip to England from 1526 to 1528, he was protected and patronized by Thomas More, before becoming the King's Painter to Henry VIII.

His portrayals of English courtiers and politicians, German merchants and craftsmen operating from the City of London, and foreign ambassadors visiting the court of Henry VIII afford us a fascinating insight into the times of King Hal.

More than a century was to pass in the same City of London before its coffee houses were the site of the first insurance companies.

Today, Chubb is very happy to be able to bring this exhibition to a wider audience in Toronto particularly, and in Canada generally.

R. T. VAN GIESON
President, Chubb Insurance Company of Canada

Preface

The drawings by Holbein and Leonardo da Vinci in the Royal Library at Windsor Castle are the most famous works in the Royal Collection of drawings, watercolours and prints. In 1977/78 the Holbein drawings (totalling eighty in number) were remounted, several layers of old backing paper were removed, some old tears were repaired and each drawing was encapsulated between two pieces of acrylic sheeting. This process meant that, given suitable atmospheric conditions and lighting, these superb works could safely be exhibited. Seventy of the drawings were shown in London at The Queen's Gallery, Buckingham Palace in 1978/79 and subsequently at the J. Paul Getty Museum, California (1982) and at the Pierpont Morgan Library, New York (1983). The selection of fifty drawings which is the subject of the present exhibition was first seen at the Museum of Fine Arts, Houston in 1987 and was displayed at the Kunsthalle, Hamburg, and the Kunstmuseum, Basel earlier this year.

The appeal and interest of these drawings is enormous for a number of different reasons. Not only are their artistic qualities self-evidently stunning; but as a group their historic importance is also easily apparent. Although the drawings are 450 years old and have inevitably suffered during the intervening years, the vividness of expression of the characters portrayed and, for example, the transparent quality of the skintone, are superb. The outstanding quality of these works is even more remarkable when one realises that of the drawings now exhibited, it is thought that only one (No. 38) was executed solely as a finished work of art in its own right. The others were primarily preparatory works for oil paintings of which a few are held in the Royal Collection (e.g. Nos 9, 19 and 40) and elsewhere, but over half of which have not survived.

A particular appeal which this set of Holbeins has in greater measure, for example, than the Leonardo da Vinci drawings in the Royal Collection, is their relevance to and, in effect, their depiction of the British history of that period. Although born in Germany and subsequently domiciled in Basel, Holbein lived in England from the age of 28 till his death aged 45, except for a single period of four years. Holbein became Court Painter to King Henry VIII and was also a close friend of Sir Thomas More. His time in England (1526–28 and 1532–43) was particularly dramatic in terms of religion, foreign policy, court politics, and King Henry's personal and marital relations. It has been estimated that in the course of his work in England he portrayed over one fifth of the English peerage, in addition to numerous other non-aristocratic members of English society.

Through the characters he so vividly drew, we therefore have a fascinating picture of the dramatis personae of a period which saw King Henry's final break with the Papacy, his establishing himself as head of the Church of England (with the help, for example, of William Warham, Archbishop of Canterbury, No. 11), his execution of those who resisted him (such as Thomas More, No. 2; and John Fisher, No. 10), and his sequence of wives (including Jane Seymour, No. 26; and Anne Boleyn, No. 27). Many of the other characters portrayed by Holbein in these drawings were gentlemen or ladies of the King's Court who were closely involved with the dramatic events of the period.

Particular credit and thanks for the preparation of this catalogue and the exhibition are due to Jane Roberts, Curator of the Print Room, and to Julia Baxter and Theresa-Mary Morton, Exhibitions Officers, in the Royal Library, Windsor Castle.

It has been a great pleasure to work with the Art Gallery of Ontario on the arrangements for this exhibition. We worked together previously on the exhibition of Leonardo da Vinci's studies for the Last Supper. Those twenty drawings from the Royal Library were shown in the Art Gallery of Ontario in 1984. And it is since 1985 that we have been discussing the possibility of the current Holbein exhibition. It is most gratifying that it is now taking place.

OLIVER EVERETT
Librarian, Windsor Castle

Acknowledgements

This book is very largely based on the work of two people: Sir Karl Parker, with whose catalogue of the Windsor Holbein drawings (first published in 1945) all subsequent studies must begin, and Dr Susan Foister, whose introductory essay to the facsimile edition of the same drawings (published in 1983) is the most substantial contribution to Holbein drawing studies in recent years. Dr Foister has helped at all stages in the planning of the present exhibition, and most generously agreed to read the catalogue text in draft form. My thanks to her are multifarious. Maryan Ainsworth, whose study of the relationship between the drawings and the related paintings is eagerly awaited, most kindly agreed to check my entries for the relevant drawings in this catalogue and to allow me to quote her unpublished conclusions concerning Nos 18, 25, 34 and 37. A preliminary account of her findings is included in M. W. Ainsworth and M. Faries, 'Northern Renaissance Paintings: the discovery of invention', *The Bulletin of the St Louis Art Museum,* n.s., XVIII, No. 1, 1986, pp. 23–37. I have received help and encouragement from a large number of other people, including the following: Nicolas Barker, Giulia Bartrum, Grace Holmes, Elizabeth Lane, Francis Russell, Hubertus Schulte Herbruggen and Olivia Winterton. Colleagues in the Royal Library and the Lord Chamberlain's Office have been extremely generous in their patience and assistance, as have my own family.

Material in the Royal Collection is reproduced by gracious permission of Her Majesty Queen Elizabeth II. The comparative illustrations included on p. 14 and within the entries for Nos 8, 11, 41 and 46 are reproduced by generous permission respectively of the Dean and Canons of Windsor, the Lord St Oswald, the Dowager Marchioness of Cholmondeley, Lord Astor of Hever, the Marquess of Tavistock and the Trustees of the Bedford Estates and the Earl of Bradford. Vertue's tracing related to No. 41 is on view at Sudeley Castle, Winchcombe, Gloucestershire. Reproductions of other works in public collections have also been kindly permitted, as follows. The catalogue numbers are given in parentheses following the location, in each case: Basel, Öffentliche Kunstsammlung (Nos 1 and 9); Berlin, Kupferstichkabinett SMPK (KdZ 36 and 2507: No. 12 and p. 9); Boston, Massachusetts, Isabella Stewart Gardner Museum (No. 34); Cambridge, Syndics of the Fitzwilliam Museum (No. 39); Dresden, Staatliche Kunstsammlungen (No. 38); Florence, Archivi Alinari (No. 35 and p. 10); Frankfurt, Städelsches Kunstinstitut (No. 49); Krakow, Muzeum Narodowe (No. 7); London, British Library (No. 24); London, British Museum, Department of Prints and Drawings (Nos 13 and 45); London, National Gallery (No. 29); London, Victoria and Albert Museum (No. 44: on loan from the Mercers' Company); New York, Frick Collection (No. 3); New York, Metropolitan Museum of Art (Bequest of Benjamin Altman, 1913; 14.40.646: No. 37; Jules S. Bache Collection, 1949; 49.7.28: No. 18); Paris, Documentation Photographique de la Réunion des Musées Nationaux (No. 11); Philadelphia Museum of Art, John G. Johnson Collection (Inv. No. 35: No. 38); Vienna, Kunsthistorisches Museum (No. 26); Washington, National Gallery of Art, Andrew W. Mellon Collection (No. 25).

Introduction

I *The Artist*

Hans Holbein, the artist responsible for all the works in this exhibition, was born in Augsburg (southern Germany) in 1497/98, the second son of an artist of the same name. Both his father, Hans the Elder (who died in 1524), and his brother Ambrosius (who died c. 1519) were active as painters, draughtsmen and designers. The father's skill as portraitist is aptly demonstrated in his study of Ambrosius and Hans the Younger in 1511 in the Kupferstichkabinett of the SMPK, Berlin. At this date Hans the Elder was doubtless already teaching his sons the rudiments of their art. By 1516 both brothers had settled in Basel. Hans worked there for most of the next decade, producing religious paintings, altarpieces, designs for stained glass, and painting the façades of some of the most prominent houses in the city. He became a member of the painters' guild in 1519, and in the following year was elected chamber master of the guild and became a citizen of Basel. Through his work in providing designs for book illustrations, he met the writers and scholars who resided in or visited the town. In 1523 Holbein painted two portraits of the great scholar Erasmus, one of which was despatched to England for William Warham (No. 11), who held the key offices of both Archbishop of Canterbury and Lord Chancellor.

HANS HOLBEIN THE ELDER: the artist's sons Ambrosius and Hans the Younger (metalpoint; Berlin, SMPK, Kupferstichkabinett, KdZ 2507)

England came to play an increasingly important part in Holbein's life, largely as a result of the fervour of religious feeling in Basel. From 1529 the iconoclasts destroyed many of his early religious works, but several years earlier there were disturbances which upset the stability that is a normal prerequisite to patronage of the arts. Following Holbein's travels through France in 1523–24, on 29th August 1526 Erasmus wrote from Basel to his fellow scholar Pieter Gillis in Antwerp to inform him that 'The arts are freezing here; [Holbein] is on his way to England to pick up a few angels [i.e. coins].' The artist delivered this letter to Gillis on his way through Antwerp and by 18th December of the same year Thomas More, the first great English humanist and future Lord Chancellor, was

WENCESLAUS HOLLAR after HOLBEIN: Holbein's self-portrait, 1543 (etching; Parthey 1418)

HANS HOLBEIN THE YOUNGER: self-portrait, 1543 (chalk with bodycolour, pen and ink; Florence, Galleria degli Uffizi)

able to write to Erasmus: 'Your painter, my dear Erasmus, is a wonderful artist, but I am afraid that he may not find England such a fruitful and fertile land as he had hoped; however, I will do what I can, so that he shall not find it all barren'.

Thomas More's role in protecting and patronizing Holbein during his first visit to England, from 1526 to 1528, is best illustrated with reference to the lost painting of More's family, for which Nos 1–8 are preparatory. As a large-scale group portrait it was a novelty not only in English art, but also in Holbein's *oeuvre* and (as an independent rather than a mural painting) in post-classical art as a whole. Other works dating from this first English visit include the portrait of Archbishop Warham (see No. 11), who had been the recipient of one of Holbein's 1523 portraits of Erasmus. The portraits of Sir Henry and Lady Guildford (see No. 9) from these same years introduce us to the circle of courtiers and administrators working directly for the English King, Henry VIII, whose paid servant Holbein later became. It is possible, however, that the decorations arranged by Guildford (in his role as Comptroller of the Royal Household) for the entertainment of the French embassy in 1527 were also the work of Holbein, for a 'Master Hans' was paid for carrying them out.

The circumstances leading to Holbein's (temporary) return to Basel from 1528 to 1532 are not known, but his wife and children had apparently remained there throughout the artist's travels. Soon after his arrival in Basel the artist purchased for his family a large house overlooking the Rhine, and acquired the adjoining house as well in 1531. Very few certain works date from these transitional years, when the political and religious climate in Basel was, if anything, even less conducive to artistic production than it had been in 1526.

By July 1532 Holbein had returned to London, and dated works punctuate his residence there until his sudden death of the plague in 1543. These begin with an imposing series of dated portraits of English courtiers and politicians, German merchants and craftsmen operating from the City of London, and foreign ambassadors visiting the thriving court of Henry VIII. It is not known exactly when Holbein first entered royal service, for the Royal Chamber accounts are lost until 1537. But in 1534 Thomas Cromwell, the King's secretary, was portrayed by Holbein, and two years later the poet

Nicholas Bourbon, who had himself been portrayed by Holbein in 1535 (see No. 47), referred to the artist as 'the King's painter'. The surviving accounts from 1537 show that from that year at least Holbein received a regular salary of £30, paid quarterly, for his work as King's painter, and was doubtless expected to carry out a very large number of miscellaneous tasks in this capacity. His portraits of members of the royal family (e.g. Nos 25 and 26) would have constituted only part of his royal duties. What may have been his principal work for the King, the dynastic painting in the Privy Chamber of Whitehall Palace, is known today only from Leemput's copy (ill., p. 16). A proportion of the many surviving designs for small-scale items such as table decorations, clocks, parade daggers and jewellery, must have resulted from some of these royal commissions.

In 1538 and 1539 Holbein travelled on the continent with the principal object of recording the likenesses of prospective brides for the King (see No. 29), and he visited Basel for a brief period at this time. A banquet was held in his honour and the City Council attempted to lure him back to Basel permanently, but to no avail. At the time of the artist's death in London in 1543, his wife and family were residing in the substantial house in Basel, benefitting to a large extent from the pension granted to Holbein by the City Council in 1538. Meanwhile, Holbein's will mentions several debts and 'two chylder wich be at nurse', presumably his illegitimate offspring from an English liaison.

Holbein's importance for the later development of English art was crucial. Through his early training in Augsburg, which was one of the first towns in south Germany to feel the effects of the Italian Renaissance, Holbein was in indirect contact with Italy from the start. But it is very likely that Ambrosius and Hans Holbein actually visited Italy in connection with one of their visits to Lucerne in 1517 and 1519. Direct quotations from Italian painting appear in works such as the portrait of Cecily Heron (No. 7). Both the pose and the *sfumato* modelling presuppose a knowledge of Milanese court art, and specifically of the works of Leonardo in the late fifteenth century. In addition to the direct and indirect influence of Italian art, it is highly likely that Holbein had access to the works of Albrecht Dürer, who visited southern Germany and Basel on several occasions. Holbein's style of portrait painting thus progressed through an ever greater mastery of perspective, of *sfumato*, and of the handling of a multiplicity of still-life accompaniments, to a virtual negation of all space surrounding the head portrayed, to provide Holbein's English sitters with not only the first opportunity that most of them had ever had for ordering a portrait of themselves, but also the possibility of the finest portraits produced in England for many decades to come. Well might Bourbon comment: 'O stranger, if you desire to see nature with all the appearance of life, look on these which Holbein's hand has created.'

The small but exquisite group of portrait miniatures certainly from Holbein's hand appear stylistically to confirm Karel van Mander's statement to the effect that Holbein did not introduce the art of miniature painting to England, but instead was introduced to it in England by the Flemish artist Lucas Horenbout, who is known to have been active there before 1528. Nevertheless, in the writings of a later miniaturist, Nicholas Hilliard, the debt owed to Holbein is expressed in a charming way (*The Arte of Living,* c. 1600):

> King Henry the eight a Prince of exquisit jugment and Royall bounty, soe that of cuning stranger even the best resorted unto him, and removed from other courts to his. Amongst whom came the most excelent Painter and limner Master Haunce Holbean the greatest Master Truly in both thosse arts after the liffe that ever was, so Cuning in both together and the neatest; and therewithall a good inventor, soe compleat for all three, as I never heard of any better than hee. Yet had the King in wages for limning Divers others, but Holbean's maner of limning I have ever imitated and howld it for the best, by Reason that of truth all the rare Siences especially the arts of Carving, Painting, Goudsmiths, Imbroderers, together with the most of all the liberall Siences came first unto us from the strangers, and generally they are the best and most in number. I heard Kinsard [? Ronsard] the great French poet on a time say, that the Ilands indeed seldome bring forth any Cunning man, but when they Doe it is in high perfection; so when I hope there maie come out of this ower land such a one, this being the greatest and most famous Iland of Europe.

II *The Reign of King Henry VIII*

Because the lives and circumstances of the sitters represented in Holbein's drawings are so inextricably bound up with the character and policies of Henry VIII, a brief account of the main events of his reign, particularly insofar as these relate to the personages shown here, may be helpful. Henry was born at Greenwich in 1491, the child of Elizabeth of York and Henry VII, who had assumed the English crown following the Lancastrian victories in the Wars of the Roses. Prince Henry succeeded his father as king in 1509, and seven weeks later married Catherine of Aragon, the widow of his deceased brother Arthur. In 1512 he invaded France, and in the following year he personally led the English army to victory at the so-called Battle of the Spurs, capturing the towns of Thérouanne and Tournai. Among those campaigning in France at this time was William Fitzwilliam (No. 39), who was the same age as the young King. The following years were full of diplomatic and military passes and counter-passes resulting for a brief moment in an Anglo-French alliance. This was celebrated in 1520 by the spectacular meeting of Henry VIII of England with Francis I of France, on the 'Field of the Cloth of Gold'. Both Guildford (No. 9) and Russell (No. 41) were in attendance on the English King during these festivities. But shortly thereafter the normal state of strife resumed. Other Englishmen later portrayed by Holbein were present at the Battle of Morlaix in 1523. George Brooke (No. 48) was rewarded for his services there with a knighthood, while Russell (No. 41) lost an eye during the battle.

Meanwhile Queen Catherine of Aragon had failed to supply Henry with a longed-for son, and he had become closely involved with the beautiful and cunning Anne Boleyn. The King had hoped that his marriage to Catherine would be declared invalid by the Pope, but Rome would not agree to this, in spite of numerous embassies from both the clergy and the laity (e.g. Nos 41 and 45). As a result of this impasse Cardinal Wolsey, the King's chief adviser in all matters both lay and spiritual, fell from favour and was dismissed and disgraced. It was therefore left to Archbishop Warham (No.11) to persuade the English clergy to accept and support the King's wishes, however revolutionary. Throughout the years 1530–32 the links binding the English Church to Rome were gradually severed, and the dues that were previously paid to the Pope were eagerly collected by the King's servants and used to pay for his expensive foreign policy. The monasteries were first suppressed and then dissolved (from 1535), one of the many results of which was the transformed appearance of the House of Lords. The seventeen abbots shown seated behind the bishops in a contemporary view of Parliament of 1523 had totally disappeared by 1553.

A number of the King's closest counsellors of the 1520s, such as John Fisher (No. 10) and Thomas More (Nos 2 and 3), were unable to accept these changes of allegiance and resigned their high offices. In 1533 the King had privately married Anne Boleyn. A year later it was declared that succession to the Crown should lie with Anne's issue rather than with Catherine's (who had given birth to a daughter, Princess Mary, but no son), and more important, that the King was the sole supreme head of the newly established Church of England. Fisher's and More's refusal to swear to this led ultimately to their execution in 1535.

Wolsey and More had been succeeded in the King's confidence by Thomas Cromwell, whose body of 'new men', recruited from a rather tougher middle class than Henry's earlier officers, scoured the land in pursuit of his policies, dissolving monasteries, seizing their properties and their revenues. Two of these, Richard Rich (No. 36) and Richard Southwell (No. 35), were heavily involved in the interrogation and trial of Sir Thomas More in 1534.

Meanwhile in May 1536 Anne Boleyn was executed for her infidelity, and on the following day the King became betrothed to Jane Seymour (No. 26). It was claimed that this was the only Queen that Henry truly loved, and he was disconsolate after her death in 1537, twelve days after the birth of his long-awaited son, Prince Edward (No. 25). Following a number of attempts at luring suitable continental brides to England (in which Holbein was himself involved), Henry married the Protestant

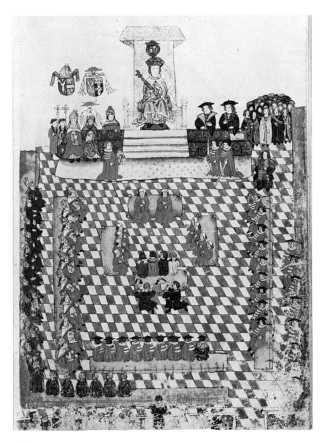

King Henry VIII in Parliament, 1523 (Wriothesley Manuscript, f. 60r)

King Edward VI in Parliament, 1553 (Dethick Manuscript; f. 1v)

Anne of Cleves as his fourth wife in 1540. The marriage was a disaster and was annulled after six months, bringing an end also to the rule of Cromwell. Henry's fifth marriage, to Catherine Howard, lasted two years and ended with her execution (for infidelity). His sixth and last wife, Catherine Parr (sister of William Parr, No. 33), outlived the King himself, who died in 1547 and was succeeded by his only son as Edward VI.

In the last years of Henry VIII's reign there was a resumption of military activity on the Continent. Boulogne was besieged in 1544, after which Philip Hoby (No. 29) was rewarded with a knighthood. John Godsalve (No. 38), who was also present at Boulogne, had to wait until 1547 for the same honour. While the British fleet was attempting to leave Portsmouth harbour to attack the French in 1545, the flagship—the *Mary Rose*—sank with the loss of all hands, including the captain, Sir George Carew (No. 46). Throughout the reign there was the additional ever-constant threat of invasion from Scotland in the north. During the Scottish campaign of 1546 Nicholas Poyntz (No. 43) served as Vice Admiral and George Brooke, Lord Cobham (No. 48) as Lieutenant General.

Meanwhile there were other problems closer to the Court. In 1546 Henry Howard, Earl of Surrey (Nos 21 and 22), and his father, the Duke of Norfolk, were arrested because it was thought, with some justification, that they planned to seize control of the young Prince Edward on the King's death. The trial proceedings were initiated by Southwell (No. 35), a childhood friend of the Earl of Surrey but a more devoted servant to the King. Both Surrey and Norfolk were found guilty of high treason, and Surrey was executed, on the day of the King's death. Norfolk, however, was pardoned in the new reign. As Prince Edward was a minor at the time of his accession, real power lay (until 1552), with his mother's brother, Lord Protector Somerset, and thereafter with Lord Protector

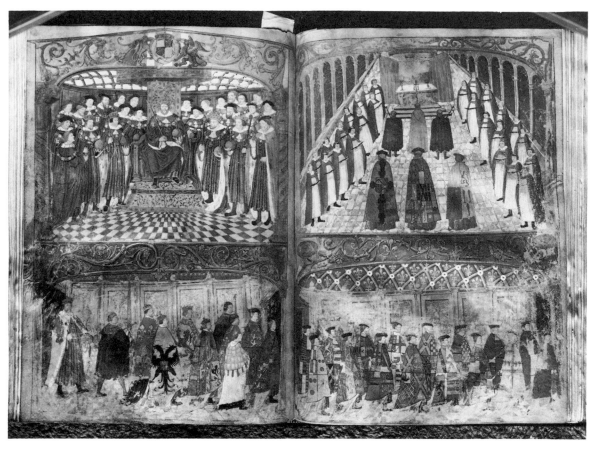

King Henry VIII and the Knights of the Garter, 1534
(Black Book of the Order of the Garter, pp. 194–95; Windsor Castle, Dean and Canons of Windsor)

Northumberland. The young King was never strong, in spite of the constant attention of the royal physicians such as William Butts (husband of No. 34), and he died aged 15 in 1553 to be succeeded by his elder sister, Mary.

Inevitably, discussions of Henry VIII's reign concentrate on his marital adventures, martial activities and religious upheavals. But other changes which took place in the reign, involving the introduction of Renaissance ideas, fashions and art forms, were of a more peaceful nature and are well illustrated by Holbein's portrait drawings that are the subject of the following pages.

III *The Sitters*

Every one of the sitters represented in this catalogue, with the possible exception of No. 12, was portrayed in England. That is not to say that they were all English by nationality, however. The fact that Holbein produced a number of oil portraits of members of the German community in London soon after his return to England in 1532, in addition to the portraits of the so-called *Ambassadors* and the *Sieur de Morette,* demonstrates that his clients (not unnaturally) included a number of foreigners. Nicholas Bourbon (No. 47) was another example of a Frenchman portrayed by Holbein during a visit to London, and the glamorous hairstyles and costumes of some of the unidentified men (such as Nos 17 and 18), together with their lack of identification (for the person responsible for adding the identities, John Cheke, is unlikely to have encountered Holbein's non-English clients), have suggested that some of them might also be foreigners.

Nevertheless, the majority of the sitters included in this selection were English and were (loosely speaking) members of the Court of King Henry VIII, whose painter Holbein became. During the artist's first visit to England he portrayed members of Sir Thomas More's family and circle (Nos 1–8), and Sir Henry Guildford (No. 9), who may have been Holbein's first court paymaster. Following his return to London in 1532 More was out of favour (owing to his refusal to agree to the King's divorce and the break with Rome), and both Guildford's and Warham's lives were drawing to a close, but Holbein appears to have had no difficulty in finding new patrons among the courtiers surrounding the throne. Among these were several who were directly involved in the condemnation of both Thomas More (Nos 2 and 3) and Cardinal Fisher (No. 10): Richard, Baron Rich (No. 36), and Lord Audley (husband of the sitter in No. 40) were both central figures in the trials leading to their executions in 1535. There is no drawn portrait of the chief instigator of these trials, Thomas Cromwell, but other 'new men' who rose through government service to find high office under Henry VIII are represented. These include figures such as John Godsalve (No. 38), and Richard Southwell (No. 35), who later supervised the dissolution of the monasteries in Norfolk.

Other important patrons of Holbein came from the older aristocratic families, such as the Howard Dukes of Norfolk. The 3rd Duke was the subject of a painted portrait by Holbein in the Royal Collection. His son, the poet Henry Howard, Earl of Surrey, was drawn and painted by Holbein on numerous occasions (e.g. Nos 21 and 22), as was his daughter Mary (No. 20), who married Henry VIII's illegitimate son, the Duke of Richmond. Henry Howard's wife Frances was also drawn by Holbein (No. 23). Anne Boleyn, the possible subject of No. 27, was the niece of the 3rd Duke of Norfolk.

Just as Holbein's first work in England had been carried out for the humanist and writer, Thomas More, to whom he had been introduced by Erasmus, so his sitters continued to be literary figures. Nicholas Bourbon and Henry Howard, Earl of Surrey, have already been mentioned. Both Sir Thomas and Lady Elyot (Nos 13 and 14) were once closely associated with the More family and were scholars in their own right. Sir Thomas Wyatt (No. 45) and Lord Vaux (No. 15) were important for both their poetry and their public office.

The opportunity to meet and portray these men and women arose because of their attendance at Court. Indeed among all the sitters represented in these drawings only one, Simon George, is totally undocumented at Court. It has been estimated that Holbein portrayed over a fifth of the English peerage (Foister, p. 33), and it can easily be demonstrated that his sitters came from a relatively closed and exclusive social group. Sir Henry Guildford (No. 9), for instance, was the first cousin of Lord Vaux (No. 15), whose sister married Thomas Strange (Parker 43). Guildford's mother married Nicholas Poyntz's (No. 43) father as her second husband, and after Sir Henry's death, Lady Guildford married Sir Gavin Carew (Parker 77), the uncle of Sir George Carew (No. 46).

At the centre both of Holbein's activity and of the court lives of his sitters was the King himself, of whom no drawing has survived. Indeed, the nearest thing to any portrait of Henry VIII by Holbein that exists in the Royal Collection is his likeness (in the guise of King Solomon) in the miniature of *Solomon and the Queen of Sheba* (No. 24). This was probably painted early in the artist's second visit to England, before the portraits of Anne Boleyn (No. 27)—if indeed it does represent her—and of her successor as Queen, Jane Seymour (No. 26). The latter's death following the birth of Prince Edward (No. 25) in 1537 led eventually to the despatch of Holbein with Sir Philip Hoby (No. 29) to take the likeness of suitable continental brides. The fact that the ravishing portrait of Christina of Denmark, Duchess of Milan, now in the National Gallery, London, was made from a drawing taken by Holbein in Brussels during a three-hour sitting, indicates the speed, efficiency and economy of line with which the artist worked, to which the drawings in this exhibition are ample testimony. The account of this sitting belongs more properly to a discussion of the artist's working methods, however.

REMIGIUS VAN LEEMPUT after HOLBEIN: Henry VII, Elizabeth of York, Henry VIII and Jane Seymour, 1667 (oil on canvas; Millar 216)

PLATE I. GRACE, LADY PARKER (No. 28; detail)

PLATE II. SIR JOHN GODSALVE (No. 38; detail)

PLATE III. An Unidentified Gentleman (No. 18; detail)

PLATE IV. AN UNIDENTIFIED LADY (No. 50; detail)

IV *History of the Drawings*

Like many aspects of the history of the Royal Collection of drawings, that relating to the Holbein portrait series is complex and incomplete. The documentary thread leading back from the twentieth to the sixteenth century has been carefully followed and recorded first by Karl Parker and more recently by Susan Foister. The ensuing account is a summary of their discussions, and for convenience relates their history forwards rather than backwards, thus somewhat blurring the silent years, when all trace of the drawings is apparently lost.

In spite of the fact that Holbein held the position of King's Painter from 1536 at least, at the time of his sudden death, in autumn 1543, his home and workshop appear to have been in the City of London rather than in the royal palace of Whitehall. His will makes no mention of his working materials or tools, and it is only by inference that we assume that the Windsor portrait drawings were among the unrecorded contents of his studio. Were it not for the fact that the collection includes a number of drawings dating from Holbein's first English stay, before he was fully integrated into the royal circle (and when he was working for patrons who by 1543 were far from acceptable to the King), we might have assumed that the drawings passed automatically to Holbein's royal patron. It is indeed possible that they can be identified with the book of patterns mentioned in Henry VIII's inventory of 1542. Another inventory, taken on the accession of Edward VI in 1547, includes 'A booke of paternes for phiosioneamyes', with a marginal annotation stating that the volume had been 'Taken by the kings Maiestie hymselfe 12° Novembre 1549' from the 'Study nexte the Kyngs olde Bedde chambre' (see Foister, p. 12).

We can be sure that the drawings once belonged to Edward VI, who had been portrayed by Holbein in his infancy (No. 25), owing to the last words of the following passage describing the series when it belonged to John, Lord Lumley, at the end of the sixteenth century: 'a great booke of Pictures doone by Haunce Holbyn of certyne Lordes, Ladyes, gentlemen and gentlewomen in King Henry the 8: his tyme, their names subscribed by Sr John Cheke Secretary to King Edward the 6 wch booke was King Edward the 6'. This statement also explains how the original identifications of the portraits were made by Sir John Cheke, Edward VI's tutor and secretary, who must therefore have been personally acquainted with the majority of the sitters. The misidentification of No. 8, and the failure to attempt to identify other early drawings, presumably arose from the fact that Cheke did not know Thomas More and members of his family. Nevertheless, the large proportion of identified drawings compares very favourably with other groups of sixteenth-century portraits, such as those at Windsor attributed to François Quesnel, for which no identifications are given (A. Blunt, *The French Drawings . . . at Windsor Castle*, London, 1945, Nos 9–19). The inscriptions which the majority of the Holbein drawings bear today are not in a sixteenth-century hand and were presumably copied from Cheke's notes on the guard papers to which the drawings were once pasted in the 'great booke'. The identifications are written on the drawings in a number of different styles. The majority bear a formal upper and lower case inscription usually at the top left corner of the sheet, written in gold (which has sometimes tarnished) over red. No. 44 bears an informal variant of this type. Other drawings, such as Nos 29, 32, 33 and 49, bear a less formal cursive inscription, as once did No. 23, although this has been deleted. The enigmatic and partially illegible words at the foot of No. 10 may be in a sixteenth-century hand, but their relevance is not known. This inscription may be related to that on the verso of the early copy of Warham's portrait (No. 11; illustrated, p. 56).

On Edward VI's death in 1553 the 'great booke' appears to have passed to the young King's Lord Chamberlain, Henry FitzAlan, 12th Earl of Arundel, on whose death in 1580 it was transferred with the rest of his collection to his son-in-law, John, Lord Lumley. When Lumley died in 1609 it is assumed that the Holbein volume passed, with the Lumley library, to Henry, Prince of Wales, and thence (in 1612) to Prince Charles, later King Charles I. The volume is next referred to, indirectly, in the inventory of King Charles's collection made in 1639, with reference to Raphael's paintings of

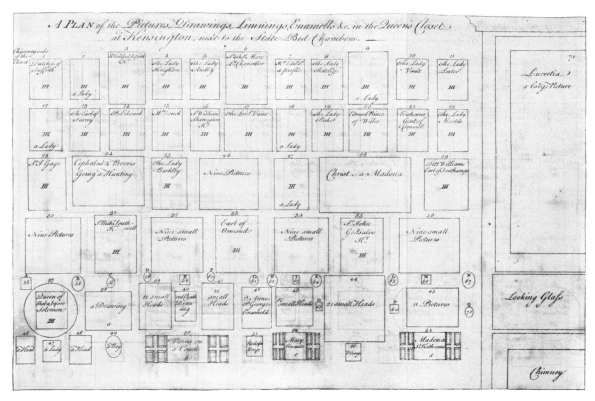

Hanging plan of a wall of the Queen's Closet, Kensington Palace (engraving; from W. Bathoe,
A Catalogue of the Collection of Pictures &c belonging to King James the Second; To which is added,
A Catalogue of the Pictures and Drawings in the Closet of the late Queen Caroline . . . and also of
the Principal Pictures in the Palace at Kensington, London, 1758; after G. Vertue, 1743)

St George and the Dragon (now in the National Gallery of Art, Washington): 'Item a little St Georg,
wch yor Matie had in Exchange of my Lord Chamberlaine for the booke of Holbins drawings wherein
manie heads were done wth Cryons wch my Lo: Chamberlaine imediatly soe soone as hee received it
of yor Matie gave it to my Lo: Marshall'. The first of these transactions, involving the exchange of the
Holbein drawings for Raphael's painting, took place c. 1627/28. It was probably Philip, 4th Earl of
Pembroke and Charles I's Lord Chamberlain from 1626 to 1641, who received the volume from the
King, and 'imediatly soe soone as hee received it' passed it on to his brother-in-law, Thomas Howard,
Earl of Arundel. During its brief transit through the Pembroke Collection it appears that one drawing
(of Lord Abergavenny) was extracted and is still to be found at Wilton House (Foister, Fig. 4).

Like Lumley and the earlier Arundel, Thomas Howard was a keen collector of sixteenth-century
art, and in particular of the works of Holbein. Among Wenceslaus Hollar's etched copies of works
in Arundel's collection are a large number of portraits by Holbein, some of which are certainly
identifiable with items in the present catalogue (e.g. Nos 8 and 24). The exact contents of the 'great
booke' at this stage are not known, however, and it is likely that some of Holbein's drawings of
English sitters which are not at Windsor may have formed part of the portrait series at this time (see
Foister, Figs 4–16 and Chapter II, *passim*).

Arundel died abroad in 1646 and his collection was then largely dispersed. The immediate fate
of the Holbein drawings is unknown. They were referred to in William Sanderson's *Graphice* (1658)
in the following words: 'Many of those pieces in the book were spoyled by the injury of time and
the ignorance of such as had it in custody'. It is possible that the drawings not at Windsor referred
to above left the collection at this time.

By 1675, however, the series of Holbein drawings now at Windsor had re-entered the Royal
Collection, for in that year Anthony Browne stated: 'The Book has long been a wanderer, but is now

happily fallen into the King's collection'. The volume was shown by Queen Mary to Constantijn Huygens the Younger in 1690 (along with the Leonardo drawings), and was then temporarily mislaid until its rediscovery in a bureau at Kensington Palace by Queen Caroline, consort of King George II. According to the list of the contents of this bureau made before 1728 (British Library Add. MS. 20101, f. 28), the drawings 'by Hans Holben' were among the items 'deliver'd for her Maj^{ys} use in ye year 1728', and are further described as 'those fram'd & hang at Richmond'. Until this point, all references to the drawings describe them as being housed in a single volume, which would doubtless have contained many useful clues as to their earlier history and context. Unfortunately (but not surprisingly) the volume has not come down to us, in contrast to the remarkable survival of the so-called 'Leoni binding' which once housed all six hundred of the Leonardo drawings now in the Royal Collection, and which is still kept in the Print Room at Windsor Castle.

Following Queen Caroline's death in 1737 the Holbein drawings were transferred from Richmond to Kensington Palace, where they were listed and their arrangement was described by George Vertue six years later. At around the same time Vertue began work on a project close to his heart, namely the publication of the drawings in engraved form. Queen Caroline had refused to agree to this scheme, for she envisaged that the drawings would suffer in the process of being copied, and 'she did not love the public enough to have [the drawings] spoilt'. But after her death Vertue set to work, tracing the outlines of the drawings onto sheets of oiled paper which must have been at least partly responsible for depositing the oil stains that are clearly visible on the surface of several of the Windsor Holbeins. Vertue's tracings of thirty-four of the Holbein drawings survive today, at Sudeley Castle, and demonstrate that the original drawings can have altered very little in the intervening years; the sheet sizes, at any rate, are extremely close. However, Vertue's scheme was ultimately abortive and no engravings were made until the very end of the century, when Francesco Bartolozzi set to work on the collection (see notes to Nos 7 and 41).

By this time the Holbein drawings had been unframed and remounted onto pages now bound up into two volumes. They were thus described by Sir William Musgrave in 1774, and (in a different arrangement) in the pages of Inventory A, which lists the Royal Collection of drawings as it existed at the end of George III's reign. During the intervening years an additional item had been added (or rather returned) to the series: the portrait of an unknown lady, cut out in silhouette, which had passed through a number of English collections until, shortly before 1792, Benjamin Way of Denham 'had the honour of receiving his Majesty's permission to add it to the Royal Collection' (No. 50). This drawing was one of the early 'strays' from the Windsor series and shares its silhouetted treatment with two others now in the British Museum and the Louvre (Foister, Figs 7 and 8). They were presumably separated from the series during the adventures of the 'great booke' in the seventeenth century.

The history of the Holbein drawings in the last two centuries has chiefly involved their mounting and remounting, their appearance in exhibitions, and the production of scholarly catalogues in which they have been discussed in considerable detail. The last remounting operation, undertaken in the Royal Library in 1977/78, involved the removal of several layers of old backing paper, the repair of old tears, and the encapsulation of each drawing between two pieces of acrylic sheeting, which serves the dual purpose of protecting the paper surface and allowing both recto and verso (and watermark) of the page to be seen without risk of damage. This was particularly relevant during the discussions leading to the photography and eventual publication of facsimile reproductions of the drawings in 1983. It has also meant that, subject to the normal restrictions concerning atmospheric conditions and lighting, exhibitions such as the one which the present catalogue accompanies could be envisaged and finally brought to fruition.

V *Purpose and Technique of the Drawings*

The manner in which the series of Holbein drawings are now kept at Windsor is naturally very different from that of earlier times. Whereas the drawings are now venerated, and rightly so, as exquisite works of art, it is likely that their primary function was as preparatory studies, made while the artist was in the presence of his subject, and used by him to work up a finished portrait in oils or, for a miniature, in tempera. The fact that the drawings have survived at all is therefore fairly surprising, when numerous similar preliminary studies must have been destroyed once they had served their purpose.

However, it is curious to note that of the fifty drawings in this exhibition, finished portraits (whether painted or printed) survive for only around half. Conversely, very few preparatory drawings relating to Holbein's oil portraits have survived. For the portraits of members of the German Steelyard (such as Derich Born and Hans of Antwerp), portrayed by the artist soon after his return to England in 1532, no drawings are known.

In the absence of evidence to the contrary, we must assume that the drawings at Windsor and elsewhere, formerly housed in the 'great booke', were gathered together in Holbein's studio at the time of his death. Their survival was thus assured, but their interest was greatly enriched soon after by Sir John Cheke's addition of identifying inscriptions. We assume that the drawings were in the artist's studio because there would seem to be no very good reason for them to be anywhere else. It is unlikely in the extreme that they were gathered together by some precocious drawings collector from the families of the respective sitters. Only one drawing, that of Sir John Godsalve (No. 38), has any pretensions to being considered as a finished work of art in its own right. However, it appears that it has always been kept with the other (preparatory) studies, so it is natural to discuss it alongside those drawings.

The relationship of drawing to oil painting, in those cases where both survive, is the subject of several detailed and on-going studies, in particular by Dr Maryan Ainsworth of the Metropolitan Museum of Art, New York. Dr Ainsworth has noted that although the one Windsor drawing in which the outlines are pricked (No. 3) is closely related to the oil painting in New York, the pouncing marks revealed in infra-red reflectography of the picture do not conform to the pricked lines of the drawing. In a few cases (e.g. Nos 11, 18, 34 and 37) it has been possible to demonstrate that the facial dimensions of drawing and painting are virtually identical, but the precise method of transfer from the drawn to the painted surface is still unknown. And thirdly in this list of uncertainties it is sometimes the case that where a painting corresponds very closely to the related drawing, the painting is unlikely to be the product of Holbein's own brush. This is particularly evident with such oft-repeated subjects as the portrait of Queen Jane Seymour (No. 26).

We have few contemporary accounts of the artist's working methods. One of the most precious is the report sent back to England from Brussels following the visit of Holbein and Hoby to interview and take the likeness of Christina of Denmark, who was at the time being considered as a possible bride for Henry VIII. The finished portrait, now in the National Gallery, London, was worked up on the basis of a three-hour sitting. Because of its size, it is highly unlikely that Holbein had the London panel in Brussels, and much more probable that the finished painting was worked up in England, following the artist's return. Holbein's preparatory work for a painting was entirely profes-sional. He worked quickly, efficiently, and with an economy of line that has ensured that his portraits are as alive today as they were in the past. Unlike other portraits of the time, they appear to be of people full of life and character, hence their enduring fascination.

Holbein employed a variety of different techniques to achieve these effects. In some cases he economised with his time and energy. Instead of colouring and texturing an area of the drawing with the correct shade, Holbein would make a note of the colour and texture on his drawing (e.g. Nos 15 and 21). Likewise, where an ornate pattern was included on the head-dress or on other parts of the clothing or jewels, Holbein would carefully work up one or more elements of the design and leave it as understood that the pattern would repeat itself (e.g. Nos 33, 42 and 50).

It has often been suggested that Holbein availed himself of a tracing device to assist in the taking of likenesses, once his London practice had become firmly established (Parker, pp. 30–31 and Fig. VIII). It is known that other Northern artists of the time (such as Dürer) made use of such aids, and it is highly likely that Holbein did so too. Indeed, the poor quality of late drawings such as Nos 36 and 46 could perhaps thereby be explained. The possibility of the addition of ink lines to these and other drawings by later retouchers has also been the matter of much discussion. Any final conclusions on this topic must be made as a result of a close study of the under-drawing to the related painted portraits. For instance it appears that in a drawing such as No. 18 the sharp chalk lines around the nose and mouth were only added after the rest of the drawing had been completed, as a final gesture of simplification, and that these shorthand and even crude lines were transferred (presumably via an intervening sheet of carbon paper) onto the panel to be painted, as the bare outlines onto which the oil glazes would later be applied, and from which the finished image would finally emerge.

The normal medium employed by Northern draughtsmen working c. 1500 was ink on paper, which would often have been coated with a coloured chalky preparation. Metalpoint was sometimes used alongside ink. Black, white and red coloured chalks and charcoal gradually came into use, as did watercolour. All the above media can be seen in the works of Dürer and Cranach. It is known that Holbein himself began to use coloured chalks following his visit to France in 1524. His portraits of members of the More family (Nos 1–8), drawn between 1526 and 1528, show a considerable mastery of this medium. They further reveal the availability of a much wider chalk colour range than we would otherwise have assumed, and one which has consequently suggested to critics that much of the coloured chalk was added long after Holbein's death. Early literary sources demonstrate that a number of other fifteenth- and sixteenth-century draughtsmen, both north and south of the Alps, used coloured chalks. Jean Fouquet's study of *Jouvenal des Ursins* in Berlin is probably the only portrait in coloured chalks to survive from before 1500. Like Holbein's drawings it was made in preparation for an oil painting, which has also happily survived (Paris, Louvre). Fouquet's example was followed by Holbein's contemporary, Jean Clouet, and then by that artist's son François Clouet, in a series of chalk portrait drawings of members of the French court. In Italy the earliest surviving instance of the complete mastery of coloured chalk is found in the work of Federico Barocci. His studies, in a technique more typical of the French eighteenth century than of the Italian Renaissance, were evidently dependent on the (now almost entirely lost) drawings in the same media by Leonardo and Correggio.

The coloured chalk drawings of Holbein's's first English period, applied to uncoated cream paper, are exceptional in the artist's work. A possible explanation is that although high quality paper was freely available in England, albeit imported from the Continent (see Appendix), the materials from which the coloured coating was made were not. Both before and after this visit, Holbein's portraits tend to be drawn on a flesh-coloured priming, using a combination of media: ink applied with pen or brush, metalpoint, chalks, and rarely watercolour. The use of the subtle pink shade for the priming successfully provides the middle ground for the modelling of the facial features, with the addition of darker shades (of chalk or ink) for the shadows, and of white chalk or paint for the highlights. It is likely that much of the chalk modelling on the drawings has disappeared during the intervening 450 years, but even on studies such as Lady Richmond (No. 20) and Mary Zouche (No. 31), enough survives for one to make out the main features of the face. When the more permanent medium of ink was used, as in Holbein's drawn copy of the More family group in Basel (illustrated on p. 30), the lifelike qualities of the portraits were evidently unmistakable to Holbein's contemporaries. Erasmus, to whom this portrait had been sent, commented: 'Holbein has represented the whole family so skilfully that if I had been present I could not have seen them better'.

CATALOGUE

1

SIR JOHN MORE

Black and coloured chalks. 351 × 273 mm. Inscribed in tarnished gold over red: *Iudge More Sr Tho: Mores Father.* Watermark: type A (Briquet 12863)

Nos 1–8 were drawn at the time of Holbein's preparatory work for his group portrait of the family of Sir Thomas More, c. 1527–28. The appearance of this painting, which is thought to have been destroyed in a fire at Kremsier Castle in 1752, is known from written descriptions and drawn and painted copies (Rowlands, cat. no. L.10). Holbein's own drawing of the group is in the Öffentliche Kunstsammlung, Basel. This was almost certainly the representation of the family on which Erasmus commented (in a letter to Thomas More's daughter, Margaret Roper) in 1529: 'Holbein has represented the whole family so skilfully that if I had been present I could not have seen them better'. The drawing was later annotated by Nicholas Kratzer (the royal astronomer and mathematician) with the names and ages of the sitters at the time of the painting. Other notes on the drawing (to the effect that Alice More should sit rather than kneel, and that the musical instruments should be moved), indicate that work on the painting was not finalised at this point. It is generally thought that these notes are in Holbein's own hand. Of the various later copies of the painting, that in oil at Nostell Priory (measuring 2.49 × 3.99 m) is probably the most reliable. It is dated 1592 and signed LOCKEY. It was presumably painted by Rowland Lockey (d. 1616) for William Roper's son. Holbein's original painting is known to have measured 9 by 12 feet (i.e. 2.75 × 3.55 m) and to have been painted in tempera on linen. A long held belief of the Winn family, who own the Nostell painting through direct descent from Sir Thomas More, is that it was started in the studio of Holbein and finished at a later date by Lockey. Tests carried out by the University of Arizona on samples of the canvas and the pigment substantiate this as a possibility.

The most precious records of the appearance of members of the More family, and also therefore of Holbein's lost painting, are the eight portrait drawings in the Royal Collection, which relate to seven of the ten personages shown in the foreground of the Basel drawing. No drawings have survived for the figures of Sir Thomas's second wife, Alice More, of his daughter Margaret Roper, or of Henry Patenson, the More family's jester. In common with other drawings dating from Holbein's first English visit, the More family studies are all executed in coloured chalks on uncoated cream paper.

Sir Thomas's father, Sir John More, was seated in the group painting to the left of his son, with Margaret Giggs and Anne Cresacre standing behind him at either side. His age is given on the Basel drawing as 75. He is thought to have been born c. 1451, the son of William More, a baker and citizen of London. John More was married three times, first (in 1474) to Agnes Graunger, the daughter of a prominent London citizen, who bore him six children, of whom Thomas was the second child and the eldest son. John More rose through the legal profession to become Sergeant at Law (1503), Judge of the Common Pleas (1518) and of the King's Bench (1523), in which capacity he may have been represented in the Wriothesley manuscript illumination illustrated on p. 13. During his later years he lived in Thomas More's house in Chelsea, where he was portrayed by Holbein. He died in 1530, and was described in Sir Thomas's epitaph as 'civilis, suavis, innocens, mitis, misericors, aequus et integer' (civil, pleasant, innocent, gentle, compassionate, impartial and honest).

(Parker 1; QG 3; RL 12224)

HANS HOLBEIN THE YOUNGER: the family of Sir Thomas More
(pen and ink; Basel, Kupferstichkabinett der Öffentlichen Kunstsammlung)

ROWLAND LOCKEY after HOLBEIN: the family of Sir Thomas More, 1592
(oil on canvas; Nostell Priory)

CAT. 1 (detail)

2

SIR THOMAS MORE

Black and coloured chalks with watercolour and metal-point. 376 × 255 mm (with an old fold-line across the lower half of the sheet). Inscribed in pen and ink, in a cursive hand: *Sier Thomas Mooer.* Watermark: type A (Briquet 12863)

Thomas More was the crucial influence in Holbein's English career, and perhaps the noblest and most enlightened figure of Henry VIII's reign. He was in touch with the group of humanists for whom Holbein had worked in Basel, and was the recipient of a letter of introduction written for the artist by Erasmus. It is assumed that Holbein visited More soon after his arrival in England in 1526, and that the group portrait of More's family was commenced soon after. Two portrait drawings by Holbein of Sir Thomas have survived in the Royal Collection (Nos 2 and 3). The appearance of the sitter in the present drawing (No. 2) is closer to that indicated in the Basel group drawing than in No. 3, although the latter is superior in many ways. The flicked-up ends of shoulder-length hair, and the somewhat hunched position of the shoulders, with the neck barely indicated, occur in No. 2 and in the Basel drawing, but not in No. 3 and the Frick Collection portrait to which it is related. The unusual technique of the present drawing, and in particular the use of wash in the cap, have given rise to doubts over its attribution. It is surely an authentic piece, however. There remains the possibility that the wash was added later.

According to the inscription on the Basel drawing, Thomas More was 50 years old at the time of the group painting. He was born in 1477/78, the second child and eldest son of John More (No. 1) and Agnes Graunger. At the age of 12 he entered the household of John Morton, Archbishop of Canterbury (and later Cardinal), who recognised the boy's considerable talents and sent him to the University of Oxford. His studies at Oxford (c. 1492–94) and at the Inns of Court prepared him for a highly successful career as a lawyer, diplomat and man of letters. He was in correspondence with Erasmus from the late 1490s and entertained the scholar during his visit to England in 1509–11. Erasmus wrote his famous satire the *Moriae Encomium* (In Praise of Folly) in 1509 while staying at More's house and dedicated the work to his friend. Erasmus's correspondence provides many fascinating insights into the life at More's houses in London and Chelsea, but he confessed that he was not competent to describe More's many-sided character. Sir Thomas's own best-known literary work, *Utopia*, was written c. 1515–16, and propounded the writer's theories of an ideal society.

Meanwhile, following his entry to Parliament in 1504, More's public career had progressed with a royal mission to Flanders in 1515, membership of the King's Council in 1517, appointment as Speaker in Parliament in 1523 and as Lord Chancellor (in succession to Wolsey) in 1529. As Speaker he is shown, from behind, in the centre of the lower margin of the picture of the 1523 Parliament in the Wriothesley Garter Book (illustrated p. 13). During the following years More became increasingly unhappy about the King's planned divorce and in May 1532 resigned the Lord Chancellorship on the putative grounds of ill-health. Following his refusal to take the Oath on the Act of Succession (which acknowledged the monarch as supreme head of the English Church), he was committed to the Tower of London on 17th April 1534. There he was interrogated by Thomas Cromwell and his agent Richard Rich (No. 36), in the presence of Southwell (No. 35). As a result of their perjured evidence, he was later charged with treason and condemned to death. He was beheaded on 6th July 1535, having proclaimed that he was 'the King's good servant, but God's first'. Thomas More was beatified in 1886 and canonised in 1935.

Contemporaries described the devout and scholarly home life of Thomas More, which was also well recorded in the lost group portrait. He was twice married, firstly to Jane Colt (before 1505), who bore him four children: Margaret (born 1505, married William Roper), Elizabeth (No. 5; born 1506, married William Dauncey), Cecily (No. 7; born 1507, married Giles Heron), and John (No. 4; born c. 1509, married Anne Cresacre). Following Jane's death in 1511, More remarried. His second wife, the widow Alice Middleton, is shown kneeling at a *prie-dieu* at far right in the Basel group drawing. She is known to have outlived More. In addition to Thomas More's own children, other young people were welcomed into the family circle, which Erasmus described as 'Plato's Academy on a Christian footing'. Margaret Giggs (No. 8) was More's adopted daughter, while Giles Heron (who in 1525 married More's youngest daughter, Cecily) and Anne Cresacre (who in 1529 married his only son, John) were both wards of Sir Thomas. William Roper, who married More's best-loved eldest daughter Margaret (not represented among the Windsor drawings), and John Clement, who married Margaret Giggs, were both members of More's household.

(Parker 2; QG 2; RL 12225)

3

SIR THOMAS MORE

Black and coloured chalks. The outlines pricked for transfer. 397 × 299 mm. Inscribed in tarnished gold over red: *Tho: Moor Ld Chancelour.* Watermark: type B (Briquet 1827)

In spite of its somewhat worn surface, and the pricking of outlines, this drawing remains one of the most compelling images from Holbein's hand. It is more closely related to Holbein's independent oil portrait of More in the Frick Collection (Rowlands, cat. no. 27) than to the group portrait for which No. 2 instead appears to have been preparatory. The Frick portrait is dated 1527, and was evidently being worked on at the same time as the group painting. X-radiography of the panel at the Frick (measuring 749 × 603 mm) reveals that a number of minor changes were made between the under-drawing (which corresponds approximately with No. 3) and the completion of the finished painting. In her recent (unpublished) study of the relationship between Holbein's drawings and the related oil paintings, Dr Maryan Ainsworth has found that the dots followed in the under-drawing of the Frick panel do not in fact correspond to those on No. 3. The gaze of the eyes and the position of the hands were adjusted between under-drawing and painting (Foister, p. 22, and Figs 49 and 50).

Apart from the cartoon fragment of the figure of Henry VIII (now in the National Portrait Gallery, London), this is the only instance of outline-pricking in Holbein's surviving *oeuvre*. Although none of the outlines of pricked drawing and oil painting correspond exactly, the shape of the drawn contours is very closely followed in the Frick painting, with a few exceptions. For instance, the line of the chain is shown as a narrow cord in the drawing but as a clear version of the collar SS, ending with the parliamentary grilles and with a pendant Tudor rose, in the painting.

It is possible that Holbein also painted an independent oil portrait of More's wife, Alice, as a pair to the Frick painting. The portrait of Lady More formerly at Corsham Court (measuring 366 × 269 mm; Rowlands, cat. no. R. 16, Pl. 227) does not appear to be by Holbein himself, and is anyway considerably smaller in format than the Frick panel. No drawn portrait of Alice More is known.

(Parker 3; QG 1; RL 12268)

HANS HOLBEIN THE YOUNGER: Sir Thomas More, 1527 (oil on panel; New York, Frick Collection)

CAT. 3 *verso*

Tho: Moor L: Chancelour

4

JOHN MORE THE YOUNGER

Black and coloured chalks.   381 × 281 mm.   Inscribed
in gold over red: *Iohn More S:r Thomas Mores Son*. Annotated by the artist, in black chalk: *lipfarb brun* (brown
complexion)

This drawing is a study for the upper part of the figure of
John More in the group portrait, in which he is shown
standing to the right of the seated figure of his father, Sir
Thomas. There, as here, he is depicted reading, but the
shallow cap shown in the drawing was evidently omitted
in the painting.

Kratzer's inscription on the Basel drawing gives John
More's age as 19, but his exact date of birth is unknown.
He was the fourth and last child and only son of Thomas
More by his first wife, Jane Colt. He was perhaps less
gifted than his elder sisters, but certainly not feeble-
minded as has sometimes been suggested. Erasmus dedicated his translation of Aristotle to him in 1531 and described him as a youth of high hopes. In 1527 he became
betrothed to his father's ward, Anne Cresacre (No. 6),
then aged 13. They married in 1529, shortly after Holbein's family group was completed. In his last letter, More
wrote to Margaret Roper: 'I pray you at time convenient
recommend me to my good son John More. I liked well
his natural fashion. Our Lord bless him and his good wife
my loving daughter, to whom I pray him be good as he
hath great cause.' At the time of Sir Thomas's imprison-
ment and condemnation, John More was also committed
to the Tower but was later released. He was at first implicated in, but then pardoned for, the involvement in a
plot against Archbishop Cranmer in 1543. He died in
1547. His grandson, Cresacre More (1572–1649), wrote
the first imprinted English biography of Sir Thomas
(c. 1631), which long remained the chief source for his
life.

In No. 4 there is a notable contrast between the densely
worked modelling of the facial features and the very free
black chalk drawing of the arm, hand and book across the
lower part of the sheet. The shadows are indicated by
broad areas of cross-hatching, the direction of the shading
lines (from top left to bottom right) clearly demonstrating
that Holbein was left-handed.

(Parker 6; QG 7; RL 12226)

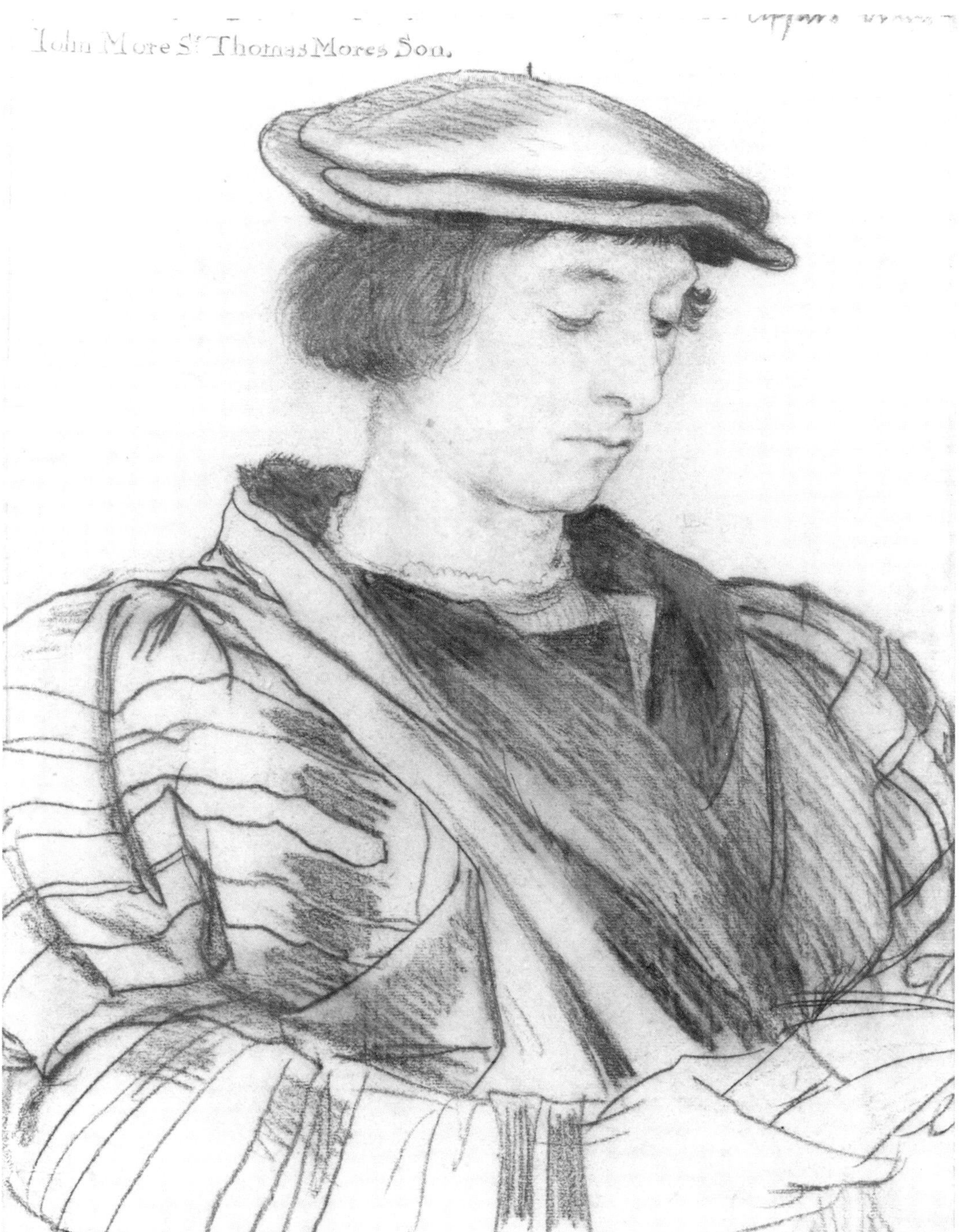
Iohn More Sr Thomas Mores Son.

5

ELIZABETH DAUNCEY

Black and coloured chalks.   367 × 259 mm.   Inscribed
(erroneously) in tarnished gold over red: *The Lady Barkley.*
Annotated by the artist in black chalk: *rot* (red)

This drawing is clearly a portrait study of the figure at the
far left of the Basel group drawing, who is identified in
the inscription as Elizabeth Dauncey, the 21-year-old
daughter of Thomas More. The title inscribed on No. 5
is certainly wrong.
   Elizabeth was the second daughter of Thomas More. In
1525, on the same day and in the same church, she and
her younger sister Cecily (No. 7) shared a marriage cere-
mony. Elizabeth's husband was William Dauncey (son of
Sir John Dauncey), Knight of the Body to Henry VIII
and Privy Councillor. Both William Dauncey and Cecily's
husband, Giles Heron, sat in the Reformation Parliament
of 1529. Dauncey was imprisoned following More's arrest
but was subsequently released.

(Parker 4; QG 10; RL 12228)

The Lady Barkley.

6

ANNE CRESACRE

Black and coloured chalks.   373 × 267 mm.
Watermark: type A (Briquet 12863)

Anne Cresacre was included in the More family group
portrait as the future wife of Thomas More's only son,
John (No. 4). Her age is given as 15 in Kratzer's annotations on the Basel drawing. The only child of Edward
Cresacre, of Barnborough (Yorkshire), while still an infant
she became one of Thomas More's many wards. As such,
she was brought up and educated with the More children,
and in 1527 became betrothed to John, who was four
years her senior. Following their marriage in 1529 she
bore him eight children. John More predeceased her (in
1547), and Anne later remarried, to George West. She
died in 1577.
   Whereas Anne was evidently drawn by Holbein while
seated on a high-backed chair, in the finished picture she
stood in the background, to the left of Sir Thomas, facing
her future husband, who stood to his right.

(Parker 7; QG 8; RL 12270)

7

CECILY HERON

Black and coloured chalks.   378 × 281 mm

Thomas More's third (and youngest) daughter, Cecily Heron, was shown seated at her father's feet in the Basel group drawing, in which her age is given as 20 years. In 1525 she had married one of her father's wards, Giles, son of Sir John Heron, Treasurer of the Chamber to Henry VIII. On the same day her sister Elizabeth (No. 5) had married William Dauncey. The two brothers-in-law both sat in the Reformation Parliament of 1529. Following More's disgrace, Cromwell ensured that Giles Heron was prosecuted, and in 1540 he was executed on a charge of treason, victim of the false witness of a disgruntled tenant. More's last letter, written to his daughter Margaret Roper on the eve of his execution, contains the following passage: 'Recommend me when ye may to my good daughter Cecily, whom I beseech our Lord to comfort. And I send her my blessing, and to all her children, and pray her to pray for me. I send her a handkerchief: and God comfort my good son her husband.'

The sitter was evidently expecting a baby at the time of the More family group (c. 1527/28). This fact is clearly

LEONARDO DA VINCI: lady with an ermine (Cecilia Gallerani. Oil on panel; Krakow, Muzeum Narodowe)

revealed in the Basel group drawing, while No. 7 shows in greater detail the expanding bodice which was so well suited to her condition. Whereas this fact was only noticed relatively recently (by Stella Mary Newton; see QG, p. 40), the similarity in pose between Cecily Heron and Cecilia Gallerani as portrayed by Leonardo da Vinci in Milan, c. 1483, has frequently been remarked upon. It is particularly noticeable in the Basel drawing, where the sitter's hands partly cover her stomach, in a very similar position to Cecilia Gallerani's hands, which caress an ermine.

Karl Parker commented on No. 7 in 1945 in the following terms: 'The drawing has evidently suffered greatly by retouching, particularly the left eye, the outline of the veil falling to the right shoulder, and the projection of the headdress at the left cheek. The yellow chalk of the stomacher has evidently been worked upon in a wet process.' While the latter statement is surely correct, current opinion tends to the view that there is considerably less retouching on the Holbein drawings than was previously thought.

Holbein's drawing of Cecily Heron was apparently the subject of a dispute between rival engravers at the end of the eighteenth century. A single impression of the soft-ground etching printed in colour by Frederick Christian Lewis (1779–1856) has survived, in the Royal Library. In a statement (signed and dated 1844 by A. W. Callcott, then Surveyor of Pictures in the Royal Collection), the genesis of this print is explained:

> When Bartolozzi's prints after the Holbein drawings in the Royal collection were nearly completed, Chamberlain their publisher [who also held the position of Royal Librarian] thought it might answer his purpose to give the public a smaller edition, if he could find any engraver of less celebrity, and at a smaller price, to supply Bartolozzi's place in this second series. His first application, and his only one, was to Frederick Lewis the engraver of *this* print; and in order the more effectually to test his power, he gave him the original drawing, requiring it to be rendered the full size of the original. When Lewis had completed his task, he took an impression to Chamberlain, who on seeing, its truthfulness when compared with Bartolozzi's print felt convinced that the reputation of the great work would be inevitably destroyed if the public once had the means of comparing such a faithful rendering as Lewis' with the false and mannered prints of Bartolozzi. He therefore desired Lewis to let him have the plate. As there have been no impressions seen but those few proofs which Lewis had taken for himself there is no doubt Chamberlain had the plate destroyed. *This* impression is one of those proofs, Lewis kindly gave me about 25 years ago.

Lewis, who was also responsible for engraving Turner's first experimental plate in the *Liber Studiorum*, held the unofficial position of Engraver of Drawings to several members of the Royal Family (i.e. George IV, Princess Charlotte, William IV and Queen Victoria). He was the father of both J. F. Lewis and F. C. Lewis the younger.

Francesco Bartolozzi after Holbein: Cecily Heron
(engraving)

Frederick Lewis after Holbein: Cecily Heron
(engraving)

Further details of Bartolozzi's two editions of the Windsor
Holbein series are given in A. Dyson, 'The engravings and
printing of the "Holbein Heads"', *The Library*, 6th ser.,
V, No. 3, 1983, pp. 223–36.

(Parker 5; QG 11; RL 12269)

CAT. 7 (detail)

8

MARGARET GIGGS

Black and coloured chalks. 379 × 269 mm. Inscribed (erroneously) in gold over red: *Mother Iak*. Watermark: type A (Briquet 12863)

Contrary to the evidence of the inscription, which identifies the sitter as 'Mother Jack' (said to have been Prince Edward's nurse), the appearance of this figure at the far left of the Nostell Priory copy of the More family group demonstrates that she should be identified as Margaret Giggs, Thomas More's foster daughter. In Lockey's copy she stands behind Elizabeth Dauncey (No. 5) and wears the same distinctive fur hat. In Holbein's Basel drawing, on the other hand, she is interposed between Elizabeth Dauncey and Sir John More, apparently referring him to the contents of the open book she holds. Margaret's pose and head-dress are quite different in the Basel drawing, suggesting that No. 8 may have been made after that drawing, but before the completion of the finished picture.

On the Basel drawing the age of Margaret Giggs (and of Margaret Roper) is given as 22. Margaret Giggs was a kinswoman of Thomas More, and was adopted by him and brought up with his family. Like the other More daughters, she was as well educated as any young man of her time. She became a considerable scholar in Greek, mathematics and medicine. Shortly before Holbein's group portrait was painted she had married her tutor, Dr John Clement, Court Physician from 1528 and President of the London College of Physicians. In More's last letter he wrote: 'I send now to my good daughter Clement her algorism stone, and I send her and my godson, and all hers, God's blessing and mine.' Margaret Clement was the only member of the More household to be present at Thomas More's execution in 1535. Following the accession of Edward VI in 1547, she and her husband went into exile at Louvain. They returned to England during Queen Mary's reign, but departed again under Queen Elizabeth, settling in Malines, where they lived for the remainder of their lives.

The fur cap worn by Margaret Giggs is similar, but not identical, to that worn by the *Lady with a Pet Squirrel* in

HANS HOLBEIN THE YOUNGER: lady with a squirrel (oil on panel; Houghton Hall)

WENCESLAUS HOLLAR after HOLBEIN: Margaret Giggs, 1648 (etching; Parthey 1552)

Mother Iak.

the Cholmondeley collection (Rowlands, cat. no. 28). That painting is one of the finest works from Holbein's first English visit, and is likely therefore to portray someone in the circle of Thomas More. The Cholmondeley painting is almost certainly identifiable with one recorded in the eighteenth century as bearing the name 'Mother Iak', the same as that still borne by No. 8. However, the sitters in the two portraits are not the same.

Hollar copied a very similar head to that shown in No. 8 in an etching dated 1648 (Parthey 1552). The portrait is cut below the shoulders and the sitter's clothing differs in several respects from that shown in the present drawing. It is therefore possible that Hollar was copying a (lost) painted portrait in his etching.

(Parker 8; QG 9; RL 12229)

CAT. 8 (detail)

9

SIR HENRY GUILDFORD

Black, white and coloured chalks. 383 × 294 mm. Inscribed in tarnished gold over red: *Harry Guldeford Knight*. Watermark: type B (Briquet 1827)

This drawing is a preparatory study for Holbein's oil portrait of Guildford, which is also in the Royal Collection (Rowlands, cat. no. 25). The painting (which measures 826 × 664 mm) is inscribed on a later *cartellino* with the date 1527 and the sitter's age, 49 years. A small roundel related to this portrait is in the Museum of Fine Arts, Houston (*Museum of Fine Arts, Houston: A Guide to the Collection*, Houston, 1981, p. 42, No. 78). It has been connected to the portrait of Guildford in the collection of the Earl of Arundel and to Hollar's etching (Parthey 1409; see Rowlands, cat. no. 25(a)). A lost roundel of Guildford's wife, Mary Wotton, is known from Hollar's etching (Parthey 1410). The large-scale companion portrait of Lady Guildford, also dated 1527, is in the City Art Museum, St. Louis (Rowlands, cat. no. 26). Holbein's drawing of Lady Guildford, somewhat differing in pose from the St. Louis painting, is at Basel.

Guildford's exact date of birth is unknown. He was the son of Sir Richard Guildford and is recorded in attendance on Henry VIII from early in the reign. His career may be traced through a number of minor royal functions until his knighthood in 1512 and his appointment as Master of the Horse in 1515, in which capacity he attended the King at the Field of the Cloth of Gold in 1520. In the oil portrait Guildford is shown holding the Comptroller of the Royal Household's white staff (1522–32), and wearing the collar of the Order of the Garter (1526). The outlines of the collar are only lightly indicated in the preparatory drawing. Guildford is almost certainly identifiable with one of the two figures standing behind the bench level with the King's throne in the view of the 1523 Parliament (see p. 13). In 1526 he was appointed Chamberlain of the Exchequer. He died in May 1532.

The many jousts and entertainments held during Henry VIII's reign were largely Guildford's responsibility. In 1527, the date on the oil portraits, Guildford authorised payment to a Master Hans (probably identifiable with Holbein) for work in connection with the Greenwich revels, which had been his personal responsibility.

When translating Guildford's likeness from paper to panel, Holbein somewhat elongated the facial proportions by slightly raising the cap on the forehead.

(Parker 10; QG 12; RL 12266)

HANS HOLBEIN THE YOUNGER: Sir Henry Guildford, 1527 (oil on panel; Millar 28)

HANS HOLBEIN THE YOUNGER: Lady Guildford (chalk; Basel, Kupferstichkabinett der Öffentlichen Kunstsammlung)

Harry Guldeford Knight.

10

JOHN FISHER

Black, white and coloured chalks, ink applied with pen and brush, and brown-grey watercolour wash, on pink prepared paper. 382 × 232 mm. Inscribed in pen and ink: *Il Epyscop° de resester / fo . . . . lato Il Cap° lan° 1535.* Watermark: type C (variant of Briquet 11341/42)

This haunting portrait has been identified in the old but enigmatic inscription as representing the Bishop of Rochester. The second line of the inscription is rendered incomprehensible by the illegibility of the second word. If (as is likely) this is to be read as *tagliato*, it could be translated as follows: 'The Bishop of Rochester [whose] head was cut [off in] the year 1535'. No satisfactory explanation has been proposed as to why this note on a portrait of an Englishman by a Swiss artist is written in a language other than English, German or a Swiss dialect. The Windsor Holbein drawings are not thought ever to have left England before finally settling in the Royal Collection c. 1670.

It has been pointed out to the author (in correspondence with both the late Edward Croft-Murray and Nicolas Barker) that the inscription is written in a very impure Italian (e.g. *Epyscopo* instead of *Vescovo*), and furthermore is penned in a mixture of North European and Italic letter forms:

From what one could judge by the scribe's performance in either direction, he was familiar with both characters of writing. This suggests an Englishman, writing perhaps between the end of the sixteenth and the end of the seventeenth century. If this is so, I think he was a man who knew no foreign language, even if he had copied out words in them, who was attempting to re-copy a very faded, illegible, and difficult inscription in an earlier hand, perhaps Holbein's. The two "Il"s must therefore be suspect. I think the first, in context, stands for an abbreviated form of "Johannes", but the second line totally defeats me. (N. Barker)

John Fisher, who was Bishop of Rochester from 1504, was born in 1469 and studied and later taught at Cambridge University around the turn of the century. He was appointed Chancellor of the University in 1504, the year of his translation to Rochester. Like Thomas More (who was around eight years younger than Fisher) and Warham (who was around twenty years older), Fisher was a friend and correspondent of Erasmus, who delivered a lecture at Cambridge in 1511 at Fisher's invitation. He was also a close friend of Lady Margaret Beaufort, who on her deathbed instructed her grandson, Henry VIII, to follow Fisher's advice in all things. But the young King had other ideas. His evolving scheme to divorce Catherine of Aragon and to proclaim himself head of the English Church was staunchly opposed by Fisher, who was in consequence imprisoned, attainted and later executed (on 22nd June 1535). He was able to communicate with his fellow prisoner, Sir Thomas More, during his time in the Tower, and they exchanged small gifts with one another. Shortly before his execution, Fisher was created Cardinal. He was beatified in 1886 and canonised in 1935.

There has been much discussion about the dating of this portrait. All the drawings which are securely datable to Holbein's first English period (Nos 1–9 and No. 11) are executed in chalks on uncoated cream coloured paper, whereas the drawings from after Holbein's return to England in 1532 are in ink and chalks on paper coated with a pink preparation. It is worth remembering, however, that Holbein used a pink primer for drawings prior to his first visit to England (as did his father and his brother Ambrosius), and that the priming on No. 10 is quite different from that used in other pink-primed English drawings. The relatively large scale of Fisher's portrait, and of the paper on which it was drawn, would suggest a dating during the first English visit. Parker was finally undecided about the chronology, while remarking, 'The later dating has, on the whole, rather more in its favour from a stylistic point of view.'

In the last resort, the clue to the dating will probably be found to lie in the portrait drawing itself, although time has doubtless deprived the surface of some of its original chalk modelling. Fisher was 66 years old at the time of his execution. When Holbein first departed from England in 1528, Fisher was 59, and the discussions concerning the King's divorce had some way to go before reaching a conclusion. No. 10 does not seem to show a fit and relatively contented man of 58 or 59. It could well, however, show an anxious man of 63 to 66, as Fisher would have been during the early years of Holbein's second English sojourn, from 1532.

At the time of his death, Fisher was described as follows: 'he was to the quantitie of 6 foote in height, and being therewith verie slender and leane, was nevertheless upright and well framed, straight backed, big joynted and strongly synewed. His hear by nature black . . ., his eyes longe and rounde, neither full black nor full graie, his nose of good and even proportion, somewhat wide mouthed and bigg jawed . . ., his skinne somewhat tawnie mixed with manie blew vaines' (quoted in Strong, p. 120). No painting of Fisher from Holbein's immediate circle appears to have survived. However, two early drawn copies exist, one in the National Portrait Gallery (NPG 2821), and the other in the British Museum (see Strong, p. 121).

(Parker 13; QG 15; RL 12205)

11

WILLIAM WARHAM

Black and coloured chalks, with some wash and some scraping out. 407 × 309 mm. Inscribed in gold over red: . . .: *Waramus Arch Bᵖ Cant:* Watermark: type B (Briquet 1827)

William Warham, born c. 1450, was the oldest member of the group of scholars and churchmen portrayed by Holbein during his first visit to England. Whereas John Fisher (No. 10) had close ties with the University of Cambridge, of which he was Chancellor from 1504, Warham studied and then taught at the University of Oxford, of which he was appointed Chancellor in 1506. He became acquainted with Erasmus following the latter's visit to England in 1505, and they corresponded regularly thereafter. It is known that Erasmus sent a portrait of himself by Holbein to Warham in 1524. That portrait is normally identified with the painting at Longford Castle, Wiltshire, which is dated 1523 (Rowlands, cat. no. 13). In return, Warham commissioned Holbein to paint him in a similar pose, presumably soon after the artist's arrival in London in 1526.

The present drawing was evidently made in preparation for the intended painted portrait, of which the principal version is now thought to be that in the Louvre (Rowlands, cat. no. 27). This bears an original inscription with the year 1527 and the sitter's age as 70 years (although

ANONYMOUS SIXTEENTH-CENTURY ARTIST after HOLBEIN: Archbishop Warham (chalk; London, The Lord Astor)

Warham was probably around 77 at the time). Examination of the panel on which the Louvre portrait is painted has also suggested that it was taken from the same tree as that on which the portraits of Guildford and Kratzer were painted, in 1527/28 (J. Fletcher and M. Cholmondeley Tapper, 'Hans Holbein the Younger at Antwerp and in England, 1526–28', *Apollo*, February 1983, p. 93). The poses of Erasmus and Warham in the two paintings (the one at Longford, the other in Paris) are very close indeed: the positions of body, face and hands differ only imperceptibly.

Warham's university life and contacts with scholars such as Erasmus were ultimately of less importance than his public career. After serving on various diplomatic missions in the 1490s, he was appointed Master of the Rolls in 1494. He held this position until his nomination as Keeper of the Seal and Bishop of London in 1502. The following year Warham was created Archbishop of Canterbury and Primate of England, and served in this crucial office throughout the troubled years following 1527 when 'the King's Great Matter' (i.e. his proposed divorce from Catherine of Aragon) was under discussion. He held the additional key office of Lord Chancellor from 1504 until 1515, in which year he was succeeded by Cardinal Wolsey. Warham and Wolsey are both depicted seated immediately

HANS HOLBEIN THE YOUNGER: Archbishop Warham, 1527 (oil on panel; Paris, Musée du Louvre)

Waramus Arch B^p Cant:

to the King's right in the view of the 1523 Parliament in the Wriothesley Garter Book (illustrated p. 13). Although Warham originally supported the Queen and disagreed violently with Cardinal Wolsey on many points concerning ecclesiastical authority, he was ultimately persuaded to embark on proceedings for the royal divorce. After Wolsey's death in 1529, Warham was left to persuade the English clergy to support the King's wishes. Only very shortly before his own death, on 22nd August 1532, did Warham publicly voice his opposition to the divorce. According to Thomas More, Warham devoted much of his fortune to noble causes and died in some poverty. His library was bequeathed to various Oxford colleges.

The relationship between No. 11 and the Louvre painting is very precise. The measurements of facial features in the two are extremely close. However, the method of transference used by Holbein is not known to us: the lines are not pricked (cf. No. 3), nor have they been gone around with a stylus. In spite of surface abrasions, No. 11 remains one of the finest of the Windsor series. 'The drawing is unequalled for its penetrating characterisation' (Parker).

An inferior version of this drawing was sold at Christie's, London, 4th July 1984 (lot 139). The dimensions of the head are roughly equivalent to those of No. 11, although the sheet size is larger (455 × 342 mm). The fact that both portrait drawings are on paper bearing the same watermark (Briquet 1827) would suggest that they both originated in Holbein's studio.

(Parker 12; QG 14; RL 12272)

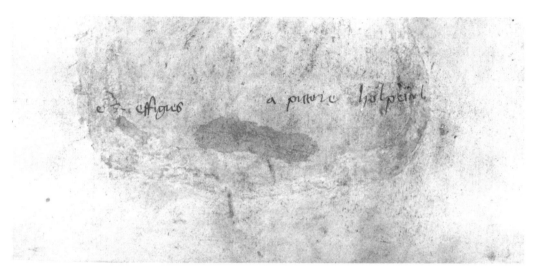

Verso of Anonymous copy of CAT. 11 (London, The Lord Astor)

CAT. 11 (detail)

12

AN UNIDENTIFIED LADY

Black and coloured chalks. 404 × 290 mm. Annotated by the artist: *atless* (silk), *dam* (damask), and (?) *rot* (red)

Although this study has apparently always formed part of the Windsor Holbein series, it may not have been drawn in England, but rather in the Low Countries while the artist was en route either to or from England. The head-dress is quite unlike that worn in any of the other Windsor drawings, and is instead very similar to those depicted by Dürer on his 1520–21 journey in the Netherlands, and in the portrait of his wife, dated 1521, in the Berlin Kupfer-stichkabinett.

The anonymity of the sitter allows us to concentrate on the construction of the head-dress, with the entrance and exit of each pin shown so deftly and simply, and the very free drawing of the folds of drapery in the sleeves and bodice. The different fabrics employed, for instance in the under-shirt (with its V-necked opening), the outer head-dress and the cap just perceptible beneath, are brilliantly depicted, as are the delicate flesh tones. 'A somewhat yellowish carnation, produced by the combined use of (?) stumped chalk with brush and water, covers the face, neck and bosom, and is graduated to suggest the transparency of the hood adjoining its vertical line on right, and of the muslin on either side of the V-shaped *decolletage*' (Parker).

(Parker 11; QG 17; RL 12273)

ALBRECHT DÜRER: the artist's wife in Netherlandish dress (metalpoint; Berlin, SMPK, Kupferstichkabinett, KdZ 36)

13

MARGARET, LADY ELYOT

Black and coloured chalks, white bodycolour and black ink on pink prepared paper. 278 × 208 mm. Inscribed in tarnished gold over red: *The Lady Eliot*. Watermark: type G (variant of Briquet 1050)

This drawing depicts Margaret, daughter of the Wiltshire gentleman Sir Maurice à Barrow, who married Thomas Elyot (No. 14) before 1520. In Thomas Stapleton's *Vita Thomae Mori*, published in Douai in 1588, it is stated that among More's 'friends and companions in the pursuit of polite literature . . . was Thomas Eliot, a well-known English writer, whose wife also gave herself to the study of literature in Sir Thomas More's school' (quoted in S. L. Lehmberg, *Sir Thomas Elyot*, Austin, 1960, p. 17). Following her husband's death in 1546, Lady Elyot married Sir James Dyer, Chief Justice of the Court of Common Pleas. She died on 26th August 1560.

No finished portraits are known of either Sir Thomas or Lady Elyot. The drawings (Nos 13 and 14) are normally thought to be the masterpieces of the early years of Holbein's second English period, c. 1532–34. The use of ink outlining combined with pink priming is the major technical distinction between the drawings of Holbein's first and second English visits. Here (and more especially in No. 31) the ink has been added with such delicacy that Holbein's responsibility for its application has seldom been queried. The much cruder application of black chalk to indicate the dark fabric of the hood must also, from the left-handed direction of the shading, be Holbein's own. It serves as a warning against too great a reliance on qualitative judgements when considering the possibility of later retouching in these drawings.

Lady Elyot's head-dress is of a type found in a number of other portraits in the Windsor series. Its structure can be explained by referring to Holbein's drawing in the British Museum (Department of Prints and Drawings, 1895-9-15-991), in which both ends are shown hanging down. In common with other ladies of her day, Lady Elyot has flicked up one end of the head-dress and placed it over the upper gable.

(Parker 14; QG 30; RL 12204)

HANS HOLBEIN THE YOUNGER: two views of a lady wearing an English hood (pen and ink; London, British Museum, Department of Prints and Drawings)

The Lady Eliot.

14

SIR THOMAS ELYOT

Black and coloured chalks, white bodycolour and black ink on pink prepared paper. 284 × 205 mm. Inscribed in gold over red: *Th: Eliott Knight.*

Thomas Elyot was born, before 1490, into a family of Wiltshire landowners. He was educated at Oxford (where he studied law, medicine and Greek), and then at the Middle Temple. He served as Clerk to the Justices of Assize from c. 1510 to 1526, and Clerk to the King's Council from c. 1523 to 1530, in which latter year he was knighted. He was sent as ambassador to Charles V in 1532. He died in 1546, at Carlton in Cambridgeshire. In his will he had made provision for 'somme image or stone sett in a wall next to my grave, wherein shalbe graven or carvide in Latten my name with the tyme of my deathe.' The grave in the parish church was once marked by brass likenesses of both Thomas and Margaret Elyot, but these have long since disappeared (Lehmberg, *op. cit.* in No. 13, p. 183).

Both Elyot and his wife (No. 13) were in close touch with Thomas More and his circle, although he was at pains to stress his loyalty to the King and to Cromwell following More's execution in 1535. Elyot's best-known work, *The Boke named the Governor,* was published in 1531. To some extent it was a logical successor to More's *Utopia* (1516), and propounded the educational theories that could be used to support the state in the new humanist world. Other works followed in the 1530s, including a Latin–English dictionary in 1538.

(Parker 15; QG 31; RL 12203)

Th: Eliott Knight.

15

THOMAS, 2ND BARON VAUX

Black and coloured chalks, white bodycolour, black ink and metalpoint on pink prepared paper. 277 × 292 mm (irregular; vertical strips added to left and right). Inscribed in gold over red: . . . [u]x. Annotated by the artist: *silbe* (silver) twice; *rot* (red), *w. sam* (for *weiss sammet,* white velvet), *Gl* (gold), *karmin* (carmine)

The very fragmentary inscription on this portrait is usually accepted as indicating Lord Vaux. Another drawing in the Royal Collection (Parker 30, measuring 289 × 203 mm) is clearly inscribed 'The Lord Vaux.', and shows a bearded man with cropped hair. It is possible, but not certain, that the same man is portrayed in both drawings. Neither drawing matches the study of Lady Vaux (No. 16) in technique, and no oil portrait of Lord Vaux is known. The existence of a painted portrait (albeit a copy) of Lady Vaux, suggests that one may also have been painted, or at least envisaged, of her husband.

Thomas Vaux was born in 1510 and succeeded his father Nicholas as 2nd Baron Vaux of Harrowden in 1523. Before this date he had married his father's ward, Elizabeth Cheney (No. 16). Lord Vaux's only official appointment was the governorship of the Isle of Jersey, which he held from January to July 1536. Prior to this date he had twice visited France (1527 and 1532), and in 1532 was dubbed a Knight of the Bath. After 1536 he retired to his estates in Northamptonshire, probably because he was unwilling to reject his Roman Catholic beliefs. The present drawing and its companion, No. 16, were probably therefore executed in or slightly before 1536. Thomas Vaux died from the plague in October 1556.

Vaux was connected with a number of Holbein's English patrons. He was a first cousin of Sir Henry Guildford (No. 9), and his sister Anne married Thomas Strange (Parker 43). A number of his poems, which are mainly elegiac and melancholy, were published posthumously in anthologies such as *Tottel's Miscellany* (1557).

The unsightly cropping of the upper corners was evidently carried out prior to Vertue's copying activities in the mid-eighteenth century, for his tracing of No. 24 at Sudeley Castle shows the drawing with the corners cut as at present.

(Parker 24; QG 56; RL 12245)

HANS HOLBEIN THE YOUNGER: Thomas, Baron Vaux (chalk with pen and ink, on pink prepared paper; Parker 30)

16

ELIZABETH, LADY VAUX

Black and coloured chalks, metalpoint, white bodycolour, and black ink applied with pen and brush on pink prepared paper. 280 × 212 mm. Inscribed in gold over red: *The Lady Vaux*. Watermark: type G (variant of Briquet 1050)

The sitter is Elizabeth, daughter of Sir Thomas Cheney, Esquire of the Body to Henry VIII. She was born c. 1505/09 and in 1516 became a ward of Nicholas, 1st Baron Vaux. Before May 1523 she had married his son and heir, Thomas Vaux (No. 15). Her death is recorded in November 1556, shortly after that of her husband.

The insensitive lines of pen and metalpoint on this drawing have naturally suggested the presence of a large amount of retouching. However, Parker noted that under the lines of the necklace, for instance, there is no trace of chalk, and that the crude shading of solid areas in the tunic, sleeves and head-dress are in a left-handed direction.

No autograph painting by Holbein of Lady Vaux has survived, but two later variants are known, one in the Royal Collection (QG 58 and Rowlands, cat. no. R. 21) and the other in the Narodni Gallery, Prague. Both show the sitter in the same position as in No. 16, but wearing a circular brooch in the centre of her bodice, just below the neckline, and holding a carnation in her right hand.

(Parker 25; QG 59; RL 12247)

ANONYMOUS ARTIST after HOLBEIN: Elizabeth, Lady Vaux (oil on panel; Millar 40)

The Lady Vaux.

17

AN UNIDENTIFIED GENTLEMAN

Black, white and coloured chalks, with black ink applied with pen and brush, on pink prepared paper. 272 × 210 mm. Annotated by the artist, in ink: *atlass* (silk), *at* (for *atlass*, silk) twice, and *S* (? satin). Watermark: type A (Briquet 12863)

No convincing identification has yet been put forward for the sitter in this portrait, although various authors have noted the somewhat un-English nature both of his facial features and of his rather stylish costume and hairstyle.

Although the annotations show that this drawing could not have been intended as a finished portrait, the face has been completed with great subtlety and detail. Much of the chalk modelling has probably been lost during the passage of time, but the facial contours, including the indications of the broken nose, are still easily read. This portrait incorporates a considerable amount of drawing (and painting) with ink, all of which must be Holbein's own. Beneath the fine, nervous pen lines of the beard are areas of black-brown wash to indicate the background fuzz. In the hair and cap a blacker ink is used, with a subtlety seldom encountered in the other portraits of the series. The drawing of the outlines of the jacket appears to have been carried out with point of brush, with a freedom that recalls the chalk drawing in the study of John More the Younger (No. 4). A date early in the second English period is probable.

Hollar's etching of this subject, in reverse, is dated 1647 (Parthey 1547). The fact that it is inscribed 'Holbein pinxit', and that the portrait is enclosed within a roundel, might suggest that the drawing was worked up into a finished painting, the present whereabouts of which are not known.

(Parker 32; QG 38; RL 12258)

WENCESLAUS HOLLAR after HOLBEIN: unknown gentleman, 1647 (etching; Parthey 1547)

18

AN UNIDENTIFIED GENTLEMAN

Black, white and coloured chalks, with some bodycolour
and ink, on pink prepared paper.   296 × 222 mm.

This drawing is the preparatory study for a circular portrait
of a man in the Metropolitan Museum, New York (Jules
S. Bache Collection), inscribed with the date 1535 and
the sitter's age as 28 years. The painting and drawing agree
in all essentials, although the painted version includes the
sitter's left hand, holding a pair of gloves, across the lower
edge of the picture and thus obscuring the broad cum-
merbund shown in the drawing. The painting also suggests that the drawn sheet has been considerably cropped
at both right and left.

Dr Ainsworth's technical examination of the New York
painting has revealed 'a more extensive under-drawing in
brush than is normally found in works by the artist (except
those from the very end of his career). The relationship of
the drawing to the under-drawing . . . shows an extremely
close match of features of the face and costume' (Dr
Maryan Ainsworth: written communication to the author,
August 1986). The same writer has observed that:

> The back of [No. 18] shows remnants of black chalk
> which appear in part to be localized to certain contour
> lines of the image . . . suggesting that these lines were
> gone over on the front side in order to effect a transfer.
> Very sharp black chalk lines appear on the front of the
> drawing reinforcing contours of the ear, collar, hat, hair
> and costume. It would seem possible, then, that features
> of the drawing were transferred (through an interleafing
> carbon-coated paper) by their reinforcement. These
> transferred lines would then have been gone over by
> brush and black pigment to form the precise under-
> drawing on the panel (*loc. cit.*).

It has recently been suggested that the Metropolitan
painting is not an autograph work, but 'by a follower, very
likely trained in Holbein's studio' (Rowlands, p. 114 and
cat. no. R. 22). Dr Ainsworth believes that the portrait is
'from the workshop of Holbein' (*loc. cit.*). The New York
roundel shares with the studio portrait of Jane Seymour
at The Hague the distinctive surface boundary surrounding the figure, which is painted on a very slightly sunken
area of the panel (Rowlands, *loc. cit.*).

(Parker 33; QG 42; RL 12259)

HANS HOLBEIN THE YOUNGER: unknown gentleman
1535 (oil on panel; New York, Metropolitan Museum of
Art, The Jules S. Bache Collection, 1949)

19

WILLIAM RESKIMER

Black, white and coloured chalks and metalpoint, on pink
prepared paper. 290 × 210 mm. Inscribed in gold over
red: *Reskemeer a Cornish Gent:*

The sitter is identifiable as William, the younger son of
John Reskimer (d. 1504/05), of Merther (near Truro),
Cornwall, who is recorded at Court continuously from
1526 until the 1540s. In the former year he was Page of
the Chamber, in 1543 he was appointed Keeper of the
Posts of the Duchy of Cornwall, and in 1546 he became
Gentleman Usher. He died before 1565. His elder brother,
John, was in attendance on Wolsey in 1521 but later
retired to the family estates in Cornwall, where he is recorded until 1546. He is therefore unlikely to be the
subject of this drawing.

No. 19 served as the preparatory study for the oil painting (measuring 464 × 337 mm) in the Royal Collection
(QG 28 and Rowlands, cat. no. 39). The outlines of the
head were transferred very exactly onto the panel, in which
the dimensions of the head are precisely as in the drawing.
The exact method of transfer is not known: the most
straightforward methods, involving a pricked outline (as
in No. 3), or running a stylus along the major lines of the
drawing, do not appear to have been employed.

In the painting the figure is extended on all sides to
include, at the bottom, both hands of the sitter, the right
one turned up rather uncomfortably to cradle the end of
Reskimer's distinctive red beard. In the background Holbein has re-used the device of vine tendrils, growing
against a flat coloured ground, as previously seen in the
1527 paintings of Sir Henry and Lady Guildford (cf. No.
9), the undated *Lady with a Pet Squirrel* (cf. No. 8), and
the portrait of Derich Born dated 1533 (Royal Collection;
QG 25 and Rowlands, cat. no. 44). These parallels may
be used to support a dating c. 1532–33 for the Reskimer
portraits.

(Parker 31; QG 29; RL 12237)

HANS HOLBEIN THE YOUNGER: William Reskimer (oil
on panel; Millar 31)

Reskeineer a Cornish   Gent:

20

MARY, DUCHESS OF RICHMOND AND SOMERSET

Black, white and coloured chalks, and black ink applied with the brush, on pink prepared paper. 266 × 199 mm. Inscribed in tarnished gold over red: *The Lady of Richmond*. Annotated in black chalk by the artist: *samet rot* (red velvet), *schwarz felbet* (black velvet), and with the initials *M, H* and *R* referring to the sitter. Watermark: type H (close to Briquet 11369)

The inscription and the initials across the lower half of the sheet identify the sitter as Mary Howard, daughter of Thomas Howard, 3rd Duke of Norfolk, and following her marriage (before 1534), wife of Henry Fitzroy, Duke of

HANS HOLBEIN THE YOUNGER: Thomas Howard, Duke of Norfolk (oil on panel; Millar 30)

Richmond, natural son of King Henry VIII and Elizabeth Blount. Mary Howard was born in 1519 and was thus married before she was 15. She was only 17 at the time of her husband's death in 1536. In 1540 she served as Lady-in-Waiting to Queen Anne of Cleves. She was an ardent Protestant, and gave evidence against both her brother Henry (Nos 21 and 22) and her father at their trials in 1547. She died in 1557.

Mary Howard's family were among Holbein's most important English patrons. Her father, Thomas Howard, 3rd Duke of Norfolk (1473–1554), was portrayed by Holbein in 1538–39, wearing the Garter collar and holding the gold baton of Earl Marshal and the white staff of Treasurer. There are numerous versions of this painting, of which the prime original appears to be that in the Royal Collection (QG 37 and Rowlands, cat. no. 68). Mary Howard's elder brother, Henry, was twice drawn (Nos 21 and 22) and at least once painted by Holbein, as was his wife Frances (No. 23). The uniformly frontal poses of Nos 20, 21 and 23 might suggest that a series of painted portraits of this type were planned (but never painted). The delicacy of modelling in the facial features, which are nowhere outlined in ink, is clearly legible in spite of the passage of time. Lady Richmond's hat, adapted from male fashions (compare that worn by her brother in No. 21), may have been intended for the hunting field. The two long shapes at the bottom of the page appear to be alternative designs, incorporating (embroidered?) initials *R*, for the underside of the cap. (Compare the decoration on the underside of Northampton's cap in No. 33.) Lady Richmond is unlikely to have worn a red velvet costume, as indicated here, following her widowhood. Just as her brother and sister-in-law were probably portrayed at around the time of their marriage in 1532, Mary Howard may have been drawn at around the time of hers to Henry Fitzroy, before 1534. For female dress of a rather similar type (including black cap and red over-dress), see the portrait of Catherine Parr in the National Portrait Gallery, London, attributed to William Scrots (NPG 4168; Strong, p. 364). This can presumably be dated to between her marriage to Henry VIII in 1543 and the King's death in 1547 (Strong).

(Parker 16; QG 35; RL 12212)

The Lady of Richmond.

21

Henry Howard, Earl of Surrey

Black, white and coloured chalks, with pen and ink, on pink prepared paper. 248 × 204 mm. Inscribed in gold over red: *Thomas Earl of Surry.*

In spite of the inscriptions on both this drawing and No. 22, there is no reason to doubt that they both represent Henry Howard, Earl of Surrey, the eldest son and heir of Thomas Howard, 3rd Duke of Norfolk. His exact date of birth is unknown, but at the time of his execution in 1547 he was around 30 years old. His early years were spent at home, where he was tutored extensively. From 1530 he was the companion of the King's natural son, Henry Fitzroy, Duke of Richmond, first at Windsor and then (1532–33) at the French Court. During this period (in 1532) Henry Howard had married Frances de Vere (No. 23), although they did not live together until 1535. Before 1534 Henry Fitzroy married the other Henry's sister Mary

Hans Holbein the Younger: Henry Howard, Earl of Surrey (oil on panel; São Paolo, Museo de Arte)

(No. 20), but he died tragically young in 1536, leaving both brother and sister distraught. It is likely that the portraits of the young Howards were made at the times of their respective marriages. In 1537 Surrey was confined at Windsor for a minor misdemeanour, but soon regained favour and was elected a Knight of the Garter in 1541. In 1542 and 1543 he was imprisoned for short periods following quarrels and disturbances, and from 1543 to 1546 he took part in campaigns in France. At the end of 1546 both Surrey and his father, the Duke of Norfolk, were charged with high treason on such pretexts as displaying royal arms on their own shields, affecting foreign dress, and employing an Italian jester. King Henry VIII's life was nearing its end and it was thought (with some justification) that the Howards were planning to seize the guardianship of Prince Edward. The information leading to their prosecution was brought together by Sir Richard Southwell (No. 35), and Mary Howard (No. 20) was persuaded to give evidence in support of the charges at the trial. Surrey was found guilty and was executed on 21st January 1547. His father's life was saved by the King's death, which occurred on the same day as Surrey's. On Norfolk's eventual death in 1554 he was succeeded by Surrey's son, Thomas Howard, born 1537/38.

Henry Howard is best known today for introducing blank verse into the English language in his translations of Virgil's *Aeneid*. He was also a notable poet in his own right, and several of his verses were published posthumously. These often recall in moving terms the happy times spent with Henry Fitzroy before his early death. With Wyatt (No. 45) he introduced the sonnet to England from Italy. Surrey's role as patron of the arts might have been better known had his ambitious new house in Norfolk, named Mount Surrey, survived. It was destroyed soon after its owner's execution. There are more portraits of Howard by Holbein and his circle than there are of any other sitter. In addition to Nos 21 and 22 there are two drawings (not by Holbein), showing a rather older man, with a wispy beard (Parker 83 and Pierpont Morgan Library, New York; see Foister, Fig. 12 and p. 4, and Strong, p. 307). The New York drawing bears an inscription in the same style as those on the majority of the Windsor drawings. It may indeed be identified among this series in Vertue's catalogue of the drawings in 1743 (see Foister, p. 9). However, it cannot be by Holbein. None of these drawings can be directly related to the oil painting in São Paolo (Rowlands, cat. no. 76).

(Parker 17; QG 32; RL 12215)

Thomas Earl of Surry.

22

HENRY HOWARD, EARL OF SURREY

Black and coloured chalks, with pen and ink, on pink prepared paper. 287 × 210 mm. Inscribed in gold over red: *Tho: Earle of Surry.* Watermark: type E (close to Briquet 12863)

For biographical details concerning the sitter, see under No. 21. It is very likely that both No. 21 and No. 22 were made c. 1532–35, at around the time of Surrey's marriage to Frances de Vere (No. 23). In spite of technical differences between them, it is clear that the two drawings of Surrey were executed at the same time and probably during the same sitting. The hairstyle is identical, as are the angle of the hat, the high collar of shirt and jacket, and the long ribbon around the neck to suspend an oval medallion (shown only in No. 22); only the viewpoint has changed. Whereas the more highly worked drawing (No. 21) is one of Holbein's masterpieces (in spite of surface damage to the back of the sheet), No. 22 is rendered somewhat pedestrian, particularly by the crude (but autograph) outlines of the hair line.

No original oil painting which accords with either of the two drawings of Surrey is known. The picture which recently appeared in the London art market (Sotheby's, London, 13th December 1978, lot 154) may have been copied from No. 21 rather than from a lost original painting. The date (1541) is probably too late. There is a painting of Surrey as a rather older man in the Museo de Arte at São Paulo, Brazil, inscribed with the sitter's age as 25 years (i.e. c. 1542; Rowlands, cat. no. 76).

(Parker 29; QG 36; RL 12216)

ho: Earle of Surry.

23

Frances, Countess of Surrey

Black, white and coloured chalks, white bodycolour and black ink, on pink prepared paper. 310 × 230 mm. Inscribed in tarnished gold over red: *The Lady Surr'y*. (A second inscription to the left of the sitter's neckline has been deleted.) Annotated by the artist: *rosa felbet* (pink velvet), *felbet* (velvet), (?) *schwarz* (black), and (?) *rot* (red). Watermark: type D (larger variant of Briquet 1457)

Frances de Vere, daughter of John, 15th Earl of Oxford, was born in 1517, around the same time as her future husband, Henry Howard, Earl of Surrey (Nos 21 and 22). In spite of Surrey's prolonged absence abroad with Henry Fitzroy, the couple married in 1532, but did not cohabit until 1535. Following her husband's execution in 1547, and before 1553, Frances Howard married Thomas Steynings. She died in 1577.

It is very likely that this drawing, and its companion No. 21, were executed near the time of the couple's marriage in 1532. No original paintings related to either portrait are known. This drawing is one of the few in the Windsor series to retain some indication (however slight) of the sitter's hands.

(Parker 18; QG 33; RL 12214)

The Lady Surry.

24

SOLOMON AND THE QUEEN OF SHEBA

Miniature painting, with pen and brush, including some use of gold paint, on vellum.   228 × 181 mm

Inscribed, in the foreground: REGINA SABA (the Queen of Sheba). On either side of the throne: BEATI VIRI TVI . . . ET BEATI SERVI HI TVI / QVI ASSISTVNT CORAM TE . . . OMNITPĒ ET AVDIVNT / SAPIENTIAM . . . TVAM; on the curtain behind Solomon: SIT DOMINVS DEVS BENEDICTVS, / CVI COMPLACIT IN TE, VT PONERET TE / SVPER THRONVM, VT ESSES REX / (CONSTITVTVS) DOMINO DEO TVO (Happy are thy men and happy are these thy servants, who stand in thy presence, and hear thy wisdom. Blessed be the Lord thy God, who delighted in thee, to set thee upon his throne, to be King [elected] by the Lord thy God). And on the steps of the throne: VICISTI FAMAM / VIRTVTIBVS TVIS (By your virtues you have exceeded your reputation).

ILLVSTRISSIMÆ ET EXELLENTISSIMÆ   HEROINÆ ALETHEIÆ MARTIÆ

WENCESLAUS HOLLAR after C. SCHUT: The apotheosis of Thomas Howard, Earl of Arundel (etching; Parthey 466)

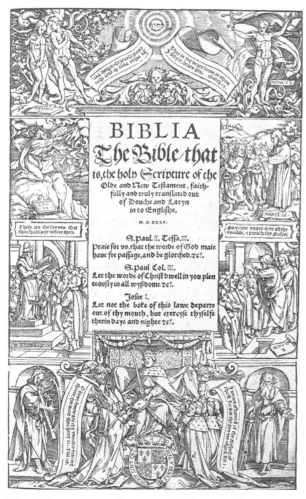

HANS HOLBEIN THE YOUNGER: Title page of the Coverdale Bible, 1535 (woodcut; London, British Library)

Detail of Hollar etching

SIT DOMINVS DEVS TVVS BENEDICTVS
CVI COMPLACIT IN TE, VT PONERET TE
SVPER THRONVM SVVM, VT ESSES REX
CONSTITVTVS DOMINO DEO TVO

VICISTI FAMAM
VIRTVTIBVS TVIS

REGINA SABA

This exquisite miniature shows Holbein working on a very much smaller scale than, and in a quite different technique from, the other items in this selection. No. 24 is akin both to the Northern tradition of manuscript illumination and to the portrait miniatures that Holbein painted for the first time during his residence in England. The degree of influence of Lucas Horenbout, who was responsible for introducing Holbein to the art of miniature painting (Karel van Mander), is unclear in works of this nature.

The texts incorporated in the composition refer to Solomon's meeting with the Queen of Sheba, and are based on II Chronicles 9 (verses 7–8). The central seated figure of King Solomon is clearly a portrait likeness of Henry VIII, shown here receiving the homage of the Queen of Sheba, who was traditionally used as a personification of the Church. By receiving her homage the King thus receives the homage of (and implicit acceptance by) the Church of England. The text further implies that the King is answerable only to God.

In both style and subject matter this miniature must date from around the time of Henry VIII's assumption of the role of Supreme Head of the English Church in 1534.

It incorporates the only autograph likeness of Henry VIII by Holbein in the Royal Collection, and possibly his first surviving portrait of the King. Holbein's frontispiece for the Coverdale Bible, which includes a portrait of Henry VIII, was published in 1535.

No. 24 is first recorded in Hollar's etching of 1642 (Parthey 74), and its reappearance four years later in Hollar's etched *Allegory on the Death of the Earl of Arundel* (Parthey 466) shows that at the time it was enclosed in a circular frame. It is highly likely that it had been presented to the King in such a format, although there is apparently no trace of it in early royal inventories. By 1688, however, it was hanging at Hampton Court. During the eighteenth century it was transferred to Kensington Palace, where it was shown—hanging in its circular frame, on the 'Chimney Side of the Closet'—by Vertue in 1743. His diagram was published by Bathoe in 1758, and is illustrated on p. 22 above. Around it were shown the drawn and painted portraits by Holbein and his contemporaries in the Royal Collection, in whose company it occupies a very natural place.

(Parker frontispiece; QG 88; Rowlands, cat. no. M. 1; RL 12188)

The inscription on the hanging cloth reads:

SIT·DOMINVS·DEVS·TVVS·BENEDICTVS·
CVI·COMPLACIT·IN·TE·VT·PONERETTE·
SVPER·THRONVM·SVVM·VT·ESSES·REX·
CONSTITVTVS)·DOMINO·DEO·TVO

The inscription on the base of the throne reads:

VICISTI·FAMAM
VIRTVTIBVS·TVIS

CAT. 24 (detail)

25

EDWARD, PRINCE OF WALES

Black and coloured chalks, and ink applied with pen and brush, on pink prepared paper. 262 × 223 mm. Inscribed in tarnished gold over red: *Edward Prince*.

The future King Edward VI was born at Hampton Court on 12th October 1537, the only (legitimate) son of Henry VIII, by his third wife Jane Seymour (No. 26), who died twelve days after his birth. Holbein's portrait was almost certainly taken in the Prince's second year, to be worked into the small panel painting (measuring 570 × 440 mm) now in the National Gallery of Art, Washington, which is usually identified with the picture of Edward presented to the King by Holbein on New Year's Day, 1539 (Rowlands, cat. no. 70). Holbein's gift was described as a 'table of the pictour of the pnce [prince's] grace'. Wearing a miniature version of the fashionable costume with feathered cap seen so frequently in Holbein's portraits, the

HANS HOLBEIN THE YOUNGER: Edward, Prince of Wales (oil on panel; Washington, D.C., National Gallery of Art, Andrew W. Mellon Collection)

young Prince raises his right hand and grasps a rattle with his left. The painting incorporates a Latin poem by Richard Morison, a government propagandist, in praise of the Prince and his royal father.

In common with many other drawings from Holbein's later years, the outlines have in places signs of reinforcement by another hand. It is probable that the drawing was never fully worked, owning to the obvious difficulties in portraying a child who had not yet reached his second birthday. Dr Maryan Ainsworth has established that the head drawn in No. 25 is slightly smaller than that painted in the Washington picture, suggesting that direct transfer was not involved. Detailed examination of the painting has shown that the under-drawing 'is of two types, a dry medium (probably black chalk) evident in the areas of the eyes and nose . . . and a liquid brush drawing in the eyes, neckline, jawline, hands, cuffs and plume of the hat. The fairly free, sketchy under-drawing is not followed exactly in the painted layers (deviations occur in the hands, for example)' (Dr Maryan Ainsworth: written communication to the author, August 1986). A second drawing at Windsor, inscribed *Edward Prince of Wales,* may well be an authentic likeness of the same sitter a few years later (Parker 71). The third drawing at Windsor inscribed as representing Edward VI is not by Holbein (Parker 85). It is normally attributed to the workshop of William Scrots (Strong, pp. 92–93).

Prince Edward had his own household from 1539, and was well tutored in the classics, the Bible, modern languages and music. His schoolmates included Henry and Charles Brandon, who were also portrayed as children by Holbein in miniature portraits in the Royal Collection (QG 85 and 86; Rowlands, cat. nos M. 10 and M. 11). From 1544 the Prince's tutor was Sir John Cheke, the man traditionally held responsible for the identifications on the Windsor Holbein drawings that were later copied onto the drawings themselves in red and gold. On 21st January 1547 Edward succeeded his father as King, but in his minority real power lay with his mother's brother, Lord Protector Somerset (until 1552), and then with Lord Protector Northumberland. The young King was not physically strong and died at the age of 15 on 6th July 1553. His piety and devotion were well-known. During his brief reign the religious reforms instituted by his father were continued so that by the time of Edward's death a very rigid form of Protestantism was widespread in England. This contrasted violently with the traditional Roman Catholic beliefs of Edward's elder half-sister, Mary, whose reign followed.

(Parker 46; QG 74; RL 12200)

Edward Prince.

26

QUEEN JANE SEYMOUR

Black and coloured chalks, with metalpoint and pen and ink, on pink prepared paper. 500 × 285 mm (with a horizontal join 65 mm from the bottom of the sheet, and old fold-lines 10 mm below this and 145 mm above this). Inscribed in gold over red: *Iane Seymour Queen*.

Although not one of the most attractive of the Windsor Holbein series, this drawing is of very considerable interest in indicating the use to which the drawings were put by the artist and his followers. It is also the most 'royal' drawing in the series, with the possible exception of the very fragmentary drawings of Jane Seymour's son, the Prince of Wales (e.g. No. 25), in which the outlines are often so faint as to be almost illegible. In the present study, much of the original chalk drawing has gone, leaving a rather 'tired' portrait with outlines often crudely worked over in metalpoint.

Jane Seymour, born c. 1509, was the daughter of Sir John Seymour (of Wolf Hall, Wiltshire) and Margaret

HANS HOLBEIN THE YOUNGER: Queen Jane Seymour (oil on panel; Vienna, Kunsthistorisches Museum)

Wentworth. She acted as Lady-in-Waiting to both Catherine of Aragon and Anne Boleyn, and by February 1536 her name was beginning to be linked romantically with the King. Anne Boleyn was condemned to death on 15th May and was executed on 19th May 1536. The following day King Henry and Jane Seymour became formally betrothed, and on 30th May they were married. At around this time the Imperial Ambassador described the Queen as 'of middle stature and no great beauty, so fair that one would rather call her pale than otherwise'. The long-awaited royal son and heir, Prince Edward (No. 25), was born on 12th October 1537, but Queen Jane died twelve days later. In the brief period of their marriage, Henry VIII had caused the initials *H* and *I* to be scattered around the newly decorated rooms at Hampton Court, to commemorate his beloved Queen. Her portrait continued to be included in royal groups long after her death, a likeness which was always based—however indirectly—on the present drawing.

The only surviving painting of Jane Seymour which is generally accepted as by Holbein himself is that in the Kunsthistorisches Museum, Vienna (654 × 407 mm; Rowlands, cat. no. 62). That painting shows the Queen three-quarter-length, and includes rather more of the lower part of the skirt and sleeves, as well as extensions to left and right, than is shown in this drawing. Although in outline the Vienna painting is clearly based on No. 26, there are a number of small discrepancies in points of detail in the jewellery. There are rather fewer such discrepancies when the drawing is set alongside the portrait of Queen Jane at the Mauritshuis, The Hague, which is a good studio work (measuring 263 × 187 mm; Rowlands, cat. no. R. 23). The latter painting shows very slightly more of the figure to left and right than in No. 26, and rather less at the base line. Re-use of the present sheet at various times suggests that the horizontal lines towards the lower edge of the sheet may have been drawn as cut-off points for pictures of different lengths. It was also presumably used as a basis for Queen Jane's portrait in Holbein's painting in the Privy Chamber, Whitehall, known today through van Leemput's copy of 1667 (Millar 216).

(Parker 39; QG 46; RL 12267)

27

QUEEN ANNE BOLEYN (?)

Black and coloured chalks on pink prepared paper. 281 × 192 mm. Inscribed in gold over red: *Anna Bollein Queen.* VERSO: heraldic sketches in black chalk. Watermark: type F (close to Briquet 11391)

The original identification of the sitter in this drawing with Queen Anne Boleyn, Henry VIII's second wife (from 1533 until her execution in 1536; his mistress from 1527), was presumably made by Sir John Cheke, tutor to Prince Edward from 1544. It has frequently been questioned, both on the grounds that Anne Boleyn is known to have been dark-haired, and because the sketches on the verso include the coat of arms of the Wyatt family. It has also been considered inherently unlikely that so elevated a personage should be depicted wearing an undercap rather than her full head-dress.

However, recent studies have reinstated the traditional identification and have claimed for Anne Boleyn a crucial role in Holbein's career at the start of his second visit to England (J. Rowlands and D. Starkey, 'An Old Tradition Reasserted . . .', *Burl. Mag.*, February 1983, pp. 88–92; Rowlands, p. 87 and *passim*). The Windsor series includes portraits of several figures connected with Anne Boleyn, such as Nicholas Bourbon (No. 47) and Lady Butts (No. 34). It is also known that Holbein collaborated with the jeweller Cornelius Heyss in a highly ornate cradle presumably made in anticipation of the birth of Queen Anne's baby, Princess Elizabeth, on 7th September 1533 (Rowlands, p. 91).

Anne Boleyn's appearance was described by several contemporaries (see Strong, p. 6). Sanudo described her as 'not one of the handsomest women in the world; she is of middle stature. Swarthy complexion, long neck, wide mouth, bosom not much raised, . . . eyes, which are black and beautiful'. An anonymous writer described her appearance at her coronation in the following terms: 'the crown became her very ill, and a wart disfigured her very much. She wore a violet velvet mantle, with a high ruff of gold thread and pearls, which conceals a swelling she has, resembling goitre.' The high neckline in the present portrait is one of the chief factors in its favour as a representation of the Queen.

Contemporary portraits certainly representing Anne Boleyn are only rarely encountered. Her total fall from grace was presumably accompanied by the destruction of all known likenesses. Her coronation medal is known only in a worn lead impression in the British Museum (illustrated in Rowlands and Starkey, *op. cit.*, Figs. 36 and 37). Roy Strong has recently reidentified the sitter in two miniatures by Lucas Horenbout (in the Buccleuch Collection and in the Royal Ontario Museum, Toronto) as Anne Boleyn (R. Strong, *Artists of the Tudor Court*, exh. cat., Victoria and Albert Museum, London, 1983, No. 14). The Toronto miniature gives the sitter's age as 25, Anne Boleyn's age at the time of her marriage to the King (if a birthdate of 1507/08 is accepted). Although Rowlands and Starkey state that 'the full face of these miniatures appears quite compatible with the profile of the Windsor drawing' (*op. cit.*, p. 91, n. 7), Horenbout's lady wears a bodice with a low neckline and does not appear to have a goitre. Meanwhile, Holbein's drawing of a lady formerly in the collection of the Earl of Bradford, but now in the British Museum, is no longer thought to have anything to do with Anne Boleyn. The most authentic of the surviving so-called likenesses appears to be that in the National Portrait Gallery, London (NPG 668, Strong, p. 5), which has little if anything in common with the present portrait.

The various heraldic devices on the verso appear to be unconnected with Anne Boleyn. The coat of arms is identified as belonging to the Wyatt family, in which case the subject of the recto could be either Sir Thomas's sister Margaret, Lady Lee, or his wife Elizabeth, sister of George Brooke, Lord Cobham (No. 48). In 1542 Elizabeth Wyatt was described by the Imperial Ambassador as 'a beautiful girl', and there were ideas that she might marry the King.

(Parker 63; QG 48; RL 12189)

CAT. 27 verso

Anna Bollein Queen.

28

GRACE, LADY PARKER

Black and coloured chalks on pink prepared paper. 298 × 208 mm. Inscribed in gold over red: *The Lady Parker.*

This charming drawing is thought to depict Grace, the daughter of Sir John Newport, who married Henry Parker, son and heir presumptive of the 10th Baron Morley (1476–1556), in 1523, when she was eight years old. Two sons were born to the Parkers, c. 1532 and 1537, and Lady Parker was present at both the christening of Prince Edward and the funeral of Jane Seymour in 1537. Henry Parker's father was a supporter of Anne Boleyn and of Princess Mary. His son predeceased him in 1553, having served as Sheriff of Hertfordshire in 1536. Henry Parker remarried before 1549, presumably following the death of his first wife, Grace, depicted in this drawing. No oil portrait related to this drawing has survived.

The head-dress, frontal gaze and youthful age of the girl sitter link this drawing with that of Mary Zouche (No. 31). There, however, the facial features have been partially strengthened by outlining, while Lady Parker is portrayed entirely in chalk. Both drawings probably date from c. 1533–36.

(Parker 73; QG 47; RL 12230)

The Lady Parker.

29

SIR PHILIP HOBY

Black and coloured chalks, on pink prepared paper. 300 × 223 mm. Inscribed in gold over red in a cursive hand: *Phillip Hobbie Knight*. Watermark: type L (Briquet 8653)

Sir Philip Hoby was a well-travelled courtier who came into contact with both Titian and Pietro Aretino during the course of his official missions abroad. He was envoy to Spain and Portugal from 1535 to 1536. On three occasions in 1538 he and Holbein respectively interviewed and took the likenesses of prospective brides for Henry VIII, following the tragic death of Jane Seymour in 1537. One of the results of these visits was Holbein's portrait of Christina of Denmark, which was taken in Brussels in March 1538, and was later worked up into the oil painting in the National Gallery, London (Rowlands, cat. no. 66).

Hoby was born in 1504/05 and married Elizabeth Stonor (No. 30) before 1540. Nos 29 and 30 were probably drawn around this time. He was a staunch Protestant and a member of Thomas Cromwell's faction. In 1538, the year of his visit to Brussels with Holbein, he was appointed Groom of the Privy Chamber, and in 1539 a Gentleman Usher. He was knighted in 1544, after the siege of Boulogne. Following the accession of Edward VI, Hoby continued to serve on diplomatic missions, and was appointed a Privy Councellor and Master of Ordance in 1552. He died in 1558.

(Parker 50; QG 67; RL 12210)

HANS HOLBEIN THE YOUNGER: Christina of Denmark, Duchess of Milan (oil on panel; London, National Gallery)

Phillip Hobbie Knight

30

Elizabeth, Lady Hoby

Black and coloured chalks and ink applied with pen and brush, on pink prepared paper. 275 × 201 mm. Inscribed in gold over red: *The Lady Hobbei*. Watermark: probably type L (Briquet 8653)

The sitter is now identified as Elizabeth Stonor, born c. 1500, the daughter of Sir Walter Stonor. She married firstly Sir William Compton, Under-Treasurer, and secondly (in 1529) Walter Walshe, a Page of the Privy Chamber, who died in March 1538. By 1540 she had married the diplomat Philip Hoby (No. 29), who would doubtless have encountered Walshe at Court, where Hoby served as a Groom of the Privy Chamber (from 1538) and Gentleman Usher (from 1539). Lady Hoby died in 1560, two years after her husband. Both husband and wife were staunch Protestants. With Lady Butts (No. 34), Lady Hoby was a member of the circle of Catherine Parr, who became Henry VIII's sixth (and last) Queen in 1543.

No painted portraits associated with either No. 29 or No. 30 are known. They were probably drawn around the time of the couple's marriage, c. 1539. The study of Lady Hoby has suffered from rubbing. Some of the ink work, particularly around the eyes, is surely too crude to be autograph.

(Parker 51; QG 68; RL 12211)

The Lady Hobbei.

31

MARY ZOUCHE

Black and coloured chalks and black ink, on prepared paper. 294 × 201 mm. Inscribed in gold over red: *M. Souch*. Annotated by the artist: *black felbet* (black velvet) Watermark: type I (Briquet 878)

The young lady in this portrait has been variously identified as the daughter (Mary), or the daughter-in-law (Joan, who died c. 1532, or Margaret), of John, Lord Zouche of Haringworth. In 1527 Mary Zouche wrote to her cousin Lord Arundel asking to be taken into royal service as her stepmother was cruel to her. A Mrs Zouche was among Queen Jane Seymour's attendants, and was granted an annuity of £10 *per annum* 'in consideration of her services to the King and the late Queen Jane'. This drawing has been dated, on the basis of style, to the start of Holbein's second English visit (c. 1532–36).

No painted portrait corresponding with this drawing is known. The large medallion lightly sketched in at the centre of the neckline of the bodice was described by Chamberlain as a representation of Perseus and Andromeda (A. B. Chamberlain, *Hans Holbein the Younger*, London, 1913, vol. II, p. 259). This is possible but not certain. Large brooches or medallions are worn by a number of Holbein's female sitters. The plain (apparently) unjewelled medallion on the present drawing is paralleled by the large circular medallion on the painted portrait of Lady Rich in New York (cf. No. 37).

(Parker 72; QG 45; RL 12252)

M Souch.

32

James Butler, 9th Earl of Wiltshire and Ormond

Black and coloured chalks, watercolour, bodycolour and ink applied with pen and brush, on pink prepared paper. 401 × 292 mm. Inscribed in gold over red (in a cursive hand: *Ormond*. Watermark: type A (Briquet 12863)

This imposing portrait, which was traditionally thought to represent Anne Boleyn's father Thomas, from 1529 Earl of Wiltshire and Ormonde (1477–1539), was convincingly identified in 1981 as showing instead the Irish peer James Butler, 9th Earl of Ormond, who for a time held the title contemporaneously with Thomas Boleyn (see David Starkey, "Holbein's Irish Sitter?", *Burl. Mag.*, CXXIII, 1981, pp. 300–303). James Butler, born before 20th July 1504, was the son of Piers Butler, the illegitimate kinsman of the 7th Earl of Ormond (died 1515) and claimant to his title and lands. He was brought up at English Court and was appointed an Esquire of the Body in 1527. In 1520 a marriage had been arranged between Butler and Anne Boleyn, in order to resolve the dispute between the Irish (Butler) and the English (Boleyn) claimants to the Ormond title. However, nothing came of the proposed match. In 1535 he became Admiral of Ireland and a Privy Councillor, and in October 1537 he attended the christening of Prince Edward (No. 25). The broad-shouldered, slashed and strapped costume worn by Ormond is very similar to that worn by Henry VIII in the Whitehall mural (and cartoon), which dated from 1537. It is possible, therefore, that James Butler was portrayed by Holbein during his visit to Court in that year. Compare, however, the dress worn by the so-called *Ambassadors* in the National Gallery, London, dating from four years earlier.

In 1539 James succeeded his father as Earl of Ormond, but he died on 28th October 1546, apparently having been poisoned during a recent visit to London.

An additional item for the iconography of Thomas Boleyn, whom this drawing was once thought to represent, is contained in the Black Book of the Order of the Garter. The pair of fully illuminated pages (pp. 194–95) contain a portrait of Thomas Boleyn, Earl of Wiltshire, walking in procession, second from the right on p. 195. He is there shown clean-shaven. He is presumably represented again among the Garter Knights surrounding King Henry VIII on the upper part of p. 194, but as these figures are uncaptioned, no specific identification appears possible (see illustration on p. 14 and E. Auerbach, 'The Black Book of the Garter', *Report of the Society of Friends of St George's*, V, 4, 1973, pp. 149–53).

(Parker 23; QG 34; RL 12263)

Ormond

33

WILLIAM PARR, 1ST MARQUIS OF NORTHAMPTON

Black and coloured chalks with white bodycolour, ink applied with pen and brush, on pink prepared paper. 317 × 211 mm. Inscribed in gold over red in a cursive hand: *William Pa[rr] / Marquis o[f] / Northamp[t]/:ton.* Annotated by the artist in black ink: *wis felbet* (white velvet), *burpor felbet* (purple velvet), *wis satin* (white satin), *w* (for *weiss,* white) five times, *Gl* (gold) twice, *gros* (size), and *MORS* (death)

William Parr was the son of Sir Thomas Parr of Kendal, who had risen to the office of Comptroller of the Royal Household before his death in 1517. He was born in 1513, and was probably therefore a year younger than his sister Catherine, who in 1543 became Henry VIII's sixth and last Queen. By that time William was himself well established at Court. He was knighted in 1537, and was created Baron Parr in 1539. In the year of his sister's marriage he became a Privy Councillor, Knight of the Garter and Earl of Essex, adding the title of Marquis of Northampton in 1547. In 1550, under King Edward VI, he was appointed Lord Great Chamberlain. As an ardent Protestant, he was imprisoned and deprived of his titles on Queen Mary's accession in 1553, but was restored to favour under Queen Elizabeth. In 1547 he married, as his second wife, Elizabeth, the daughter of George Brooke, Lord Cobham (No. 48). He died in 1571.

George Vertue recorded seeing a portrait of this sitter in the collection of Dr Meade, but it is not known whether that portrait followed the lines of the present drawing. It has been suggested that Northampton's costume (and in particular the medallion and hat badge) may be connected with that worn by the Gentleman Pensioners, of which he was appointed Captain in November 1541 or 1542. The Pensioners were a band of the King's retainers who protected him on the battlefield.

The use of ink to reinforce the outlines and the various details that are worked up in the upper left corner makes this drawing among the richest in decorative detail of the Windsor series. Parker noted that 'there are no traces whatever of preliminary chalk lines under the penwork in details of jewellery'.

(Parker 57; QG 53; RL 12231)

William S...
Marqui̇s of
Northam
ton

Rm̃ por
Holben

nẽ̃ Paen

34

MARGARET, LADY BUTTS

Black and coloured chalks with metalpoint and black ink applied with pen and brush, on pink prepared paper. 377 × 272 mm. Inscribed in gold over red: *The Lady Butts.*

Margaret Bacon, daughter of John Bacon of Cambridgeshire, was born c. 1485 and married Henry VIII's Court Physician, Sir William Butts. Both husband and wife served the royal family in various capacities. As Court Physician, Sir William was responsible for the well-being of the King, the Queen and their children. He looked after Prince Edward during his serious illness in 1541. Lady Butts is recorded in waiting to Princess Mary (whom her husband also served), but was a strict Protestant and was closely linked with Queen Catherine Parr. She died in 1547.

The drawing served as a preparatory study for Holbein's oil painting of Lady Butts, aged 57, in the Isabella Stewart Gardner Museum, Boston (Rowlands, cat. no. 81). The oil portrait of Sir William Butts, aged 59, for which no

drawing has survived, is in the same museum (*ibid.*, cat. no. 80). A pair of early copies of these portraits is split between the National Portrait Gallery and the Bacon collection (Strong, p. 334). Sir William reappears, in an identical pose (and therefore presumably based on the same preparatory study) in the group portrait of Henry VIII and the Barber-Surgeons at the Royal College of Surgeons, London (*ibid.*, cat. no. 78), commissioned in 1540. Lady Butts's portrait was reproduced (in reverse) in an etching by Wenceslaus Hollar dated 1649 (Parthey 1553).

The ink outlining around the facial features, particularly the eyes and nose, is followed very faithfully in the underdrawing of the Boston painting. This ink work, and the disappearance of most of the chalk modelling, contribute to an impression of flatness which seems to characterise much of Holbein's later draughtsmanship. The detail at the end of the V-neckline on Lady Butts's bodice is translated into a charming enamelled (?) pink flower in the painting.

Recent technical examination of the Boston painting and its relationship with No. 34 has revealed the following:

> The overlay of the drawing is nearly the exact size of the painting (perhaps some allowances should be made for shrinkage of the drawing from various restorations over time). Furthermore, the lines of the drawing are very precisely reproduced in the under-drawing of the painting. This includes features of the drawing such as the fur ball at the sitter's left shoulder and the lines of the blouse opening, which are reproduced in the under-drawing, but not in the painting itself. In other words, the drawing and the under-drawing are somewhat closer to each other than either is to the painted version (Dr Maryan Ainsworth: written communication to the author, August 1986).

Dr Ainsworth has also suggested

> that the means of transfer of these details of the sitter from the drawing to the under-drawing is likely to be by reinforcing the drawing lines with a stylus (or metalpoint). An incised line was found in the painting along the right edge of the costume at the fur collar and around the exterior contour of the torso. There probably would have been an interleafing carbon-coated sheet which would have effected the transfer. These fugitive charcoal or chalk lines would then have been gone over with the brush and black pigment to form the underdrawing for the painting (*ibid.*).

(Parker 67; QG 69; RL 12264)

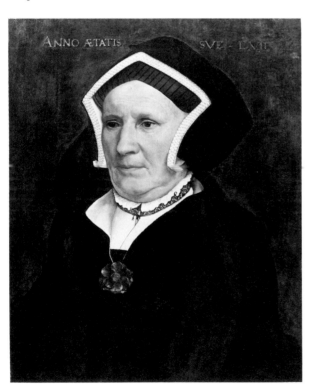

HANS HOLBEIN THE YOUNGER: Lady Butts (oil on panel; Boston, Isabella Stewart Gardner Museum)

35

SIR RICHARD SOUTHWELL

Black and coloured chalks with metalpoint and ink applied with pen and brush, on pink prepared paper.
366 × 277 mm.   Inscribed in gold over red: *Rich: Southwell Knight*. Annotated by the artist, in pen: *Die augen ein wenig gelbatt* (the eyes a little yellowish), and in chalk: [A]NNO ETTATIS SVA[E] · 33.   Watermark: type D (larger variant of Briquet 1457)

The oil painting for which this drawing is preparatory is in the Uffizi, Florence (Rowlands, cat. no. 58) and follows No. 35 very closely in all essentials, while extending the figure to half length by the inclusion of hands, and showing more of the upper arms to right and left. The painting bears an inscription to right and left of the sitter's head, extending that given on the drawing. The painted inscription allows the portrait to be dated 1536. The three blemishes on the face and neck, which Parker and all previous writers described as patched holes, are in fact very meticulous depictions of scars on Southwell's skin. The line of the back of the neck follows the inner ink line of the drawing rather than the outer chalk line. The hat badge is shown in the painting to contain a bejewelled female figure (possibly Lucretia), and Southwell wears a heavy interlinking gold chain around his neck.

Richard Southwell's activities as one of Cromwell's most loyal and unscrupulous henchmen are well documented. He was born c. 1502/03, the son of Francis Southwell, a wealthy Norfolk squire. After receiving a pardon (on payment of £1,000) for a charge of murder in 1532, he was made Sheriff of Norfolk and Suffolk in 1534. He was present in the Tower in 1535 during the interrogation by Richard Rich (No. 36) of Sir Thomas More (Nos 2 and 3), but when asked to give evidence at More's trial he replied that he had not heard the answers More had given to Rich's questions (which were falsely reported by Rich), as he was too busy removing Sir Thomas's books. His career continued to prosper thereafter, and in the following year he was appointed Receiver to the Court of Augmentations. Southwell was elected M.P. for Norfolk in 1539, received a Knighthood in 1540, and initiated the proceedings leading to the downfall of his childhood friend Henry Howard, Earl of Surrey (Nos 21 and 22),

HANS HOLBEIN THE YOUNGER: Sir Richard Southwell (oil on panel; Florence, Galleria degli Uffizi)

in 1545. He was a close associate of Thomas Cromwell and was much involved in the dissolution of the monasteries, enriching himself considerably in the process. He was a Privy Councillor under both Edward VI and Queen Mary. Southwell was imprisoned in the Fleet Jail as a Catholic in 1549–50, and was likewise out of favour under Queen Elizabeth. He died in 1564.

(Parker 38; QG 23; RL 12242)

Southwell Knight.

NNO   ETTATIS SVA
                                          ·3·

36

RICHARD, 1ST BARON RICH

Black and coloured chalks with pen and ink on pink prepared paper. 320 × 261 mm. Inscribed in gold over
red: *Rich L:^d Chancelor.* Watermark: type K (Briquet
11387)

Rich was around seven years older than Southwell (No.
35), and was equally involved as a henchman of Thomas
Cromwell in carrying out the King's wishes during the
1530s. Born c. 1496, he was appointed Solicitor-General
in 1533 and thus officiated at the trials of both Fisher
(No. 10) and More (Nos 2 and 3) in 1535. His perjured
evidence concerning his interrogation of More ensured
the latter's demise. Rich was a Member of Parliament on
several occasions, Speaker in 1536, and Chancellor of the
Court of Augmentations from 1536 to 1544. In 1547 he
was created Baron Rich and served as Lord Chancellor,
from that year to 1551. He founded Felsted School in
Essex in 1564 and died three years later. Before 1536 he
had married Elizabeth Jenks (No. 37), who died in 1558,
having reputedly borne him fifteen children.

Nos 36 and 37 were presumably produced as pendants
towards the end of Holbein's life. They were drawn on
paper bearing an identical watermark. No comparable
painted portrait of Richard Rich is now known, although
one is mentioned by Chamberlain and may have been
destroyed in 1904 (see Rowlands, *sub* cat. no. R. 26,
p. 234). No. 36 is one of the least well preserved drawings
of the whole series. The oil stain over Rich's left eye may
have been applied at the time of Vertue's traced copies in
the mid-eighteenth century.

(Parker 80; QG 75; RL 12238)

Rich L:ᵈ Chancelor.

37

ELIZABETH, LADY RICH

Black, white and coloured chalks with pen and ink and metalpoint, on pink prepared paper. 374 × 300 mm. Inscribed in gold over red: *The Lady Rich.*, and again in a cursive hand at the level of the sitter's right shoulder. Annotated by the artist: *damast* (damask), and *samet* (velvet). Watermark: type K (Briquet 11387)

The sitter was Elizabeth, daughter of William Jenks, a London spice merchant. She married the unscrupulous Richard Rich (No. 36) before 1536 and is said to have borne him fifteen children. She died in 1558. The drawing is on paper bearing the same watermark as that of its pendant, No. 36.

There are two oil portraits of Lady Rich which follow No. 37 in most essentials but extend the figure slightly at all four sides (Rowlands, cat. no. R. 26). Both are probably studio works. The painting in a West German private collection is considered the superior by Rowlands. In the version in the Metropolitan Museum, New York (Rowlands, Pl. 236), Lady Rich wears a large circular medallion of an unidentified subject.

Dr Ainsworth's technical examination of the New York painting has revealed the following:

The under-drawing in brush is extensive—all the contours of the face, its features, and the costume. The photostat overlay of the Windsor Castle drawing shows an exact alignment of all these features and a closer relationship of the two drawings to each other than to the painting where there are a few modifications of the design. The medallion has been added and the contours of the head-dress have been slightly altered, for example.

The transfer of the design from the drawing to the panel was by means of reinforcement of lines by metalpoint. This is clear from the fact that the metalpoint lines on the drawing are exactly reproduced in the brush lines of the under-drawing on the panel. No other lines of the drawing, including the reinforced pen lines, are so exactly reproduced. The transfer must have involved an interleafing carbon-coated sheet which would have deposited on the panel a fugitive carbon line, subsequently gone over with brush and black pigment or ink to form the under-drawing. It is interesting to note that

ANONYMOUS ARTIST after HOLBEIN: Lady Rich (oil on panel; New York; Metropolitan Museum of Art, Bequest of Benjamin Altman, 1913)

some lines on the drawing which are made in metalpoint alone—the cuff of the sleeve at the very bottom of the page, for example—are reproduced in the under-drawing as well. Perhaps the metalpoint was used not only to effect the transfer of the drawing but also to make corrections of the chalk drawing during the transfer process (Dr Maryan Ainsworth: written communication to the author, August 1986).

(Parker 55; QG 76; RL 12271)

The Lady Rich.

38

SIR JOHN GODSALVE

Black, white and coloured chalks, with watercolour and bodycolour, and ink applied with pen and brush on pink prepared paper. 362 × 292 mm. Inscribed in tarnished gold over black: *S⟨r⟩ Iohn Godsalve*, and again in gold in a cursive hand (to left of head).

Like various other sitters represented in this exhibition (e.g. Surrey and Wyatt), Godsalve was portrayed more than once by Holbein. Chronologically the first of the series was the double portrait of John Godsalve with his father Thomas, dated 1528, which is in the Gemäldegalerie Alte Meister in Dresden (Rowlands, cat. no. 31). The inscription on that painting identifies the elder sitter as Thomas Godsalve of Norwich, aged 47; he died in 1542. John Godsalve was born c. 1510.

The elder Godsalve was a close friend of Thomas Cromwell. In November 1531, in return for many kindnesses shown to his son, Sir Thomas sent Cromwell 'half a dozen swans of my wife's feeding'. Both father and son served as Registrar in Norwich. In 1531 John was appointed Clerk of the King's Signet and in 1532 received a grant in survivorship of the Office of Common Meter in Precious Tissues. This position must have brought him into close contact with the Hanseatic merchants for whom Holbein worked during the years immediately following his return to England in 1532. The present portrait may date from soon after. Godsalve participated in the French campaign of 1544 and was knighted in 1547. The following year he was appointed Comptroller of the Royal Mint in the Tower. He died in 1556.

This drawing is unique in the Windsor series for being a finished piece, densely worked in colour, and including *trompe l'oeil* effects (for example, the right hand resting on a ledge) such as one would expect to find in oil paintings. The normal pink preparation is scarcely visible through the blue background. The only comparable drawing to have survived is the portrait traditionally identified as Prince Edward, at Basel. The pose of the sitter in No. 38 is close, but not identical, to that in a painting in the John G. Johnson collection, Philadelphia, which is not considered to be authentic (Rowlands, cat. R. 19).

(Parker 22; QG 40; RL 12265)

ANONYMOUS ARTIST after HOLBEIN: John Godsalve (oil on panel; Philadelphia Museum of Art, John G. Johnson Collection)

HANS HOLBEIN THE YOUNGER: Thomas Godsalve and his son John, 1528 (oil on panel; Dresden, Gemäldegalerie Alte Meister)

Sr Iohn Godsalue

39

WILLIAM FITZWILLIAM 1ST EARL OF SOUTHAMPTON

Black, white and coloured chalks with metalpoint on pink prepared paper. 383 × 270 mm. Inscribed in tarnished gold over red: *Fitzwilliams Earl of Southampton*. Watermark: type A (Briquet 12863)

The sitter in this portrait held a number of important official positions during the reign of Henry VIII, whose contemporary he was. William Fitzwilliam, born c. 1490, the son of Sir Thomas Fitzwilliam, was appointed Gentleman Usher in 1509. William was himself knighted in 1513 following his participation in the military engagements against France in 1512 and 1513. During a visit to France in 1521 Fitzwilliam had his portrait taken, but complained that the artist 'did not do my portrait well . . . he made [it] in haste' (Foister, p. 3). In 1522 he was appointed Vice-Admiral, and in 1525 Treasurer of the Household. The following year he was elected a Knight of the Garter. In 1529 he became Chancellor of the Duchy of Lancaster, and in 1537, on relinquishing the post of Treasurer, he was created Earl of Southampton. He is identified as the central of the three Garter Knights seen from behind in the upper right illumination (on p. 195) in the Black Book of the Order of the Garter (1534; illustrated p. 14). From 1536 to 1540 he served as Lord High Admiral and thereafter as Lord Privy Seal. He died in 1542 on his way to fight the Scots.

The drawing may be dated with reference to the staff of Lord High Admiral which Fitzwilliam seems to hold (i.e. between 1536 and 1540). A (Garter?) collar is also indicated. Holbein's original painting after this drawing is said to have been destroyed by fire at Cowdray House in 1793. A copy survives in the Fitzwilliam Museum, Cambridge. This shows the figure full-length, with the Admiral's staff, standing against a coastal landscape. It is rather perplexingly dated 1542, the year of Southampton's death and two years after he had ceased to be Admiral. The landscape background is unlikely to have been present in Holbein's original. Other versions are in the Devonshire collection and in the Fitzwilliam family collection.

The sitter in this portrait was not related to Thomas Wriothesley, Earl of Southampton, the subject of Holbein's portrait drawing in the Louvre (Foister, Fig. 8). Wriothesley was created Earl of Southampton in 1547, an honour bestowed on him in his role as Joint Governor of the young Edward VI, in fulfilment of the (alleged) intentions of the late King, whose executor he had been. The earlier earldom of Southampton had become extinct five years before, following the death of William Fitzwilliam.

(Parker 66; QG 26; RL 12206)

ANONYMOUS ARTIST after HOLBEIN: The Earl of Southampton, 1542 (oil on panel; Cambridge, The Fitzwilliam Museum)

Fitz Williams Earl of Southampton.

40

ELIZABETH, LADY AUDLEY

Black and coloured chalks with metalpoint and pen and ink on pink prepared paper. 293 × 208 mm. Inscribed in gold over red: *The Lady Audley*. Annotated by the artist: *samet* (velvet), *rot damast* (red damask), *rot* (red), *w* (for *weiss*, white), and *Gl* (gold)

The identity of this sitter is problematic. She has been assumed to be Elizabeth, daughter of Brian Tuke (portrayed by Holbein in a portrait in Washington; Rowlands, cat. no. 64). She married George Touchet, who succeeded his father as 9th Baron Audley in 1557, considerably after Holbein's death. Susan Foister has suggested a reidentification of the sitter as Elizabeth, daughter of the 2nd Marquess of Dorset, who became the second wife of Sir Thomas Audley, More's successor as Lord Chancellor, before September 1538. Sir Thomas had been one of the King's chief tools in forcing through his religious and constitutional reforms. He was created Baron Audley of Walden later in the same year, but died in 1544. In 1549 Lady Audley remarried, to Sir George Norton; she died in 1564. Her mother, Margaret, Marchioness of Dorset, is portrayed in a very damaged drawing by Holbein at Windsor (Parker 28).

No large-scale painting following this drawing is known, but it is followed very exactly in Holbein's miniature portrait of the same lady in the Royal Collection (measuring 57 mm diameter; Rowlands, cat. M. 9). There the double row of her necklace, and the jewel-encrusted brooch in the centre of Lady Audley's bodice, are finely depicted. In common with many of the other Windsor Holbeins, the drawing seems to have been cropped at either side and at the foot, thus eliminating the shoulders and hands. A date c. 1540 has been suggested for both drawing and miniature.

(Parker 58; QG 44; RL 12191)

HANS HOLBEIN THE YOUNGER: Lady Audley (miniature)

The Lady   Audley.

Parner   vet enough

41

JOHN RUSSELL, 1ST EARL OF BEDFORD

Black, white and coloured chalks on pink prepared paper. 349 × 292 mm. Inscribed in gold over red: *I Russell Ld Privy Seale. with one Eye*

John Russell was born in Dorset c. 1486, and served at court as a Gentleman Usher under Henry VII. During the early part of Henry VIII's reign he frequently visited France, and later Italy and Spain. He was knighted c. 1513, was present at the Field of the Cloth of Gold in 1520, and accompanied Thomas Howard (later 3rd Duke of Norfolk) to France in 1522. At the battle of Morlaix during this campaign, Russell lost the use of his right eye (as mentioned in the inscription). He was appointed a Gentleman of the Privy Chamber in 1526 and sat in the Reformation Parliament three years later. In 1537 he became Comptroller of the Royal Household, and in 1539 was created Baron Russell of Chenies and elected a Knight of the Garter. From 1540 to 1542 he was Lord High Admiral of England, and was recorded as Lord Privy Seal in 1542, 1547 and 1553. He was one of the executors of

Henry VIII's will and was created Earl of Bedford in 1550. He died five years later and was succeeded by his son Francis.

No autograph painting dependent on this drawing is known, but at Woburn Abbey there is a half-length portrait of the 1st Earl of Bedford which is directly based on No. 41; it is a late copy of the Holbein portrait (Strong, p. 21). In the painting the sitter wears a Garter collar, and a black cap on top of the black skull cap in which he is portrayed in the drawing. Both the Woburn picture and the Windsor drawing appear to show the right eye intact. However, Vertue's copy of the drawing (at Sudeley Castle) subtly indicates the right eye as unseeing, suggesting that an alteration may have been made in that area of this drawing. At Woburn there is another portrait of the same sitter, also anonymous, more frontally posed and dated 1555, the year of Bedford's death (Strong, Pl. 43).

(Parker 69; QG 27; RL 12239)

GEORGE VERTUE after HOLBEIN: tracing of CAT. 41 (Sudeley Castle)

ANONYMOUS ARTIST after HOLBEIN: John Russell, Earl of Bedford (oil on panel; Woburn Abbey)

J Russell Ld Privy Seale.   with one Eye

42

AN UNIDENTIFIED LADY

Black and coloured chalks and black ink applied with pen and brush on pink prepared paper. 289 × 210 mm. Annotated by the artist: *rot* (red), *liecht rot damast* (light red damask), *rot* (red), *w* (for *weiss*, white), *s* (? for *schwarz*, black), and (?) *Gold-ornament* (on head-dress)

There is no clue to the identity of the sitter in this charming portrait. The richness of the materials and jewels would suggest a lady of some standing, and the quality of the drawing would seem to indicate a date c. 1532/34.

(Parker 61; QG 19; RL 12253)

43

SIR NICHOLAS POYNTZ

Black and coloured chalks on pink prepared paper. 281 × 182 mm. Inscribed in gold over red: *N. Poines Knight*. Watermark: type G (variant of Briquet 1050)

Nicholas Poyntz was the son of Sir Anthony Poyntz (of Iron Acton, Gloucestershire) and the nephew of John Poyntz, of whom a portrait exists in the Holbein series at Windsor (Parker 54). Nicholas was born before 1510 and was appointed Keeper of Parks in Gloucestershire in 1531. He was knighted two years later, and was Sheriff of Gloucestershire in 1536 and 1539. He was at Court for important occasions such as the christening of Edward, Prince of Wales, in 1537, and he went to meet Anne of Cleves in 1540. During the two years following he spent short periods in the Fleet prison as a result of his indebtedness, but in 1546 he was reinstated as Vice Admiral in the wars against France and Scotland. He died in 1557.

A number of pictures and miniatures relating to this drawing are known, but it is doubtful whether any are fully autograph works by Holbein.

A group of paintings, of which the best is that at Sandon Hall (Rowlands, cat. no. R. 27), give the sitter's age as 25 and the date as 1535. Such a date would agree with the style of this drawing. Two miniature copies were recently on the art market (Christie's, London, 25th November 1980, lot 70; Sotheby's, London, 7th March 1983, lot 18). The Sandon Hall painting is identifiable with the picture saved from the fire at Cowdray House, Sussex, in 1793. It is not possible to say whether it is the 'ritratto del Cavaglier Points' (thought to be by Holbein) in the collection of the Earl of Arundel. Rowlands (p. 233) states:

> The Harrowby portrait has been accepted as by Holbein by Chamberlain and Schmid. But although it is undoubtedly the best version of the portrait surviving, the style of execution, totally lacking Holbein's' vitality, makes an attribution to him untenable. Evidently it is by a talented follower working from the drawing now at Windsor (Parker 34). Holbein also drew a portrait of a relative of Sir Nicholas, John Poyntz of Alderley (Parker 54); and a portrait after this is also at Sandon Park.

(Parker 34; QG 55; RL 12234)

N Pomes   Knight.

44

JOHN COLET

Black, white and coloured chalks, ink applied with pen and brush, and metalpoint, on pink prepared paper. 267 × 203 mm. Inscribed in gold over red: *Iohn Colet Dean of St Paul's.* Watermark: type F (close to Briquet 11391)

The fact that Colet died in 1519, seven years before Holbein's first visit to England, led Parker and others to doubt the identification inscribed on this drawing. However, in 1950 F. Grossman demonstrated that Holbein was here depicting a bust of the sitter (attributed to Pietro Torrigiano), rather than the sitter himself, hence the peculiarly small scale of the head when compared to other portraits in the Windsor series (F. Grossman, 'Holbein, Torrigiano and some portraits of Dean Colet', *J.W.C.I.*, XIII, 1950, pp. 202–35).

John Colet was born c. 1466, the son of a city mercer who became Lord Mayor of London. After studying at Oxford University, he was ordained in 1498. Between 1497 and 1503 he delivered a series of lectures at Oxford in which he stressed the importance of the New Testament and criticised current Church practice. In 1505 he was appointed Dean of St Paul's Cathedral, London, and four years later he founded St Paul's School. Colet was a close friend of Thomas More and his humanist circle, and was acquainted with Erasmus. Following his death in 1519, an elaborate tomb was set up to Colet's memory in St Paul's Cathedral, London. In 1548 the monument was described as incorporating a '*depicta ad vivum effigies*' (an effigy coloured life-like) of the deceased, and this is shown to have been a half-length three-dimensional figure in the anonymous etching of Colet's monument included as page 64 of Dugdale's *History of St Paul's Cathedral* (1658). The engraving itself is dated 1656 and bears inscriptions by Hollar (Parthey 2272A). The sculptural portrait of Colet was badly damaged in the Great Fire of 1666 and is now known through plaster casts, of which the best is that in the Victoria and Albert Museum, London. The casts suggest an attribution of the original to Pietro Torrigiano, an Italian sculptor active in England from 1511 to c. 1520.

Plaster cast of bust of John Colet by PIETRO TORRIGIANO (London, The Mercers' Company on loan to the Victoria and Albert Museum)

John Colet's tomb in Old St Paul's Cathedral, 1656 (etching, Parthey 2272A; from W. Dugdale, *History of St Paul's Cathedral*, London, 1658)

John Colet. Dean of St Paul's

45

SIR THOMAS WYATT

Black, white and coloured chalks, with pen and ink, on pink prepared paper. 372 × 269 mm. Inscribed in gold over red: *Tho: Wiatt Knight*.

Sir Thomas Wyatt the poet was the son of Sir Henry Wyatt, who served as Treasurer of the Chamber to Henry VIII. He was born c. 1504 and was educated at St John's College, Cambridge. In 1524 he was appointed Clerk of the King's Jewels and three years later accompanied Sir John Russell (No. 41) on his embassy to the papal court. In 1529–30 Wyatt was High Marshall at Calais, and in 1533 he was appointed Privy Councillor. Wyatt was knighted in 1535. He was temporarily imprisoned in the Tower at the time of Anne Boleyn's execution (1536), and may have been her lover before she became Queen. He was ambassador to Charles V from 1537 to 1539, and was again temporarily imprisoned at the time of Cromwell's fall (1541). His wife Elizabeth was the sister of George Brooke, Lord Cobham (No. 48). Wyatt repudiated her for adultery in 1537. He died in 1542.

Wyatt's writings (both sacred and profane) relied heavily on his studies of foreign literature. He was largely responsible (with Surrey, No. 21) for introducing the sonnet into English literature. Their poems were among

ANONYMOUS SIXTEENTH-CENTURY ARTIST after HOLBEIN: Sir Thomas Wyatt (woodcut, from Leland's *Naeniae in mortem Thomae Viati*, 1542)

those included in *Tottel's Miscellany* (1557), together with pieces by Lord Vaux (No. 15) and others. However, Wyatt was acknowledged as the outstanding poet of his age.

Thomas Wyatt's likeness was evidently taken by Holbein more than once. He was presumably introduced to the artist by his father, whose oil portrait by Holbein is in the Louvre (Rowlands, cat. no. 29). On the basis of recent dendrochronological examinations, that painting is now thought to date from in or shortly after 1535 (E. Foucart-Walter, *Les Peintures de Hans Holbein le jeune au Louvre*, Paris, 1985, pp. 50 and 68). There are two nearly identical drawings of Thomas Wyatt at Windsor, of which No. 45 is superior. The second drawing (Parker 65), which is badly rubbed, is probably a copy of No. 45. Karl Parker suggested, very tentatively, that the copyist was Federico Zuccaro, who is stated to have made copies of Holbein's designs. this is inherently unlikely in view of the fact that Parker 65 is on paper which Holbein is known to have used (type H).

No oil painting related to these drawings is known. A second Holbein portrait showing Wyatt bareheaded in three-quarter profile within a roundel is known through various derivations (e.g. NPG 1035 and 2089, Strong, pp. 338–39), which include the woodcut published to accompany an elegy on Wyatt's death in Leland's *Naenia* (1542). Strong has suggested a date c. 1535 for No. 45, and c. 1540 for the three-quarter profile portrait. Thomas Wyatt's son, Sir Thomas the Younger (c. 1521–54) was also portrayed by Holbein, in pure profile, bareheaded and within a roundel (see Strong, pp. 340–41). The younger Wyatt, who was a close friend of Surrey (Nos 21 and 22), was executed for high treason in 1554. It may also be relevant that the elder Wyatt's wife was the sister of George Brooke, Lord Cobham, the subject of No. 48 in the present exhibition.

(Parker 64; QG 79; RL 12250)

ANONYMOUS SIXTEENTH-CENTURY ARTIST after HOLBEIN: Sir Thomas Wyatt (chalks with pen and ink; Parker 65)

Tho: Wiatt Knight.

46

Sir George Carew

Black and coloured chalks with metalpoint on pink prepared paper. 316 × 233 mm. Inscribed in tarnished
gold over red: *S G. Carow Knight*

George Carew, born c. 1505, was the eldest son of Sir
William Carew of Mohuns Ottery in Devon. He was the
nephew of Gavin Carew, whose portrait by Holbein is
also at Windsor (Parker 77), and who married as his
second wife Mary, Lady Guildford, the widow of Sir
Henry Guildford (No. 9). George Carew served as Sheriff
of Devon in 1536–37 and in 1542, during which time he
was sometimes at sea with the Navy. In 1539 he was
appointed Captain of the Tower at Ruysbank, Calais. Five
years later he became Lieutenant of the Gentlemen Pensioners and a Gentleman of the Privy Chamber. In recent
times Carew has regained his fame during the publicity
surrounding the raising of the wrecked hulk of the *Mary
Rose* from the seabed off Portsmouth. Carew was captain
of the ship and drowned with all other hands when she
foundered in 1545, while attempting to leave Portsmouth
harbour to engage the French fleet.

A painted version of this portrait, from Holbein's studio, is in the collection of the Earl of Bradford at Weston
Park (Rowlands, cat. no. R. 34). This has been cut to a
circular format (diameter 336 mm), but was originally
square. The light tone of the cap feather and of the
undershirt, buttoned up to the neck, sets a lively contrast
with the dark background and the sitter's dark beard.
Holbein's portrait probably dates from the end of the
artist's life, c. 1540/43.

(Parker 76; RL 12197)

Anonymous Artist after Holbein: Sir George Carew
(oil on panel; Weston Park)

Detail of engraving, showing the sinking of the Mary
Rose in Portsmouth Harbour

G. Vertue: *Naval Engagement in the Solent*, showing the sinking of the Mary Rose (engraving)

S G. Carow Knight

47

NICHOLAS BOURBON THE ELDER

Black, white and coloured chalks with pen and black ink, on pink prepared paper. 307 × 260 mm. Inscribed in tarnished gold over red: *Nicholas Borbonius Poeta*.

Nicholas Bourbon was born in Troyes in 1503 and became associated with members of the humanist movement such as Erasmus and Paolo Giovio, both of whom admired his Latin verse. As a Protestant, he was persecuted in France for his religious beliefs, but won the protection of Henry VIII and particularly of Anne Boleyn. In gratitude for their kindness, Bourbon visited England in 1535 to pay homage to the King and Queen. This portrait was presumably taken during the poet's English visit, for it evidently provided the basis for the woodcut portrait of Bourbon (in reverse) dated 1535. Unusually for the drawings in the Windsor series, No. 47 incorporates an alteration in the position of the hands and arms towards the lower edge of the sheet. The raised right hand holding the quill, lightly sketched in over the lowered right arm, recurs in the woodcut portrait. However, the poet's gaze is hardly directed towards the piece of paper on which he writes. The woodcut portrait was first used in books printed by Sebastian Gryphius in Lyons in 1536, including Bourbon's collected verses entitled *Nugae* (Trifles).

Following the fall of Anne Boleyn, Bourbon returned to France. On 5th September 1536 he wrote to Henry VIII's French secretary, Thomas Soulemant, asking him to send greetings to 'all with whom you know me connected by intercourse and friendship'. The list of names that follows includes Cranmer, Cromwell, Butts, Kratzer, 'my host, the King's goldsmith', Cornelius Heyss, and Holbein, 'the royal painter, the Apelles of our time' (N. Bourbon, *Paidagogeion*, Lyons, 1536, p. 27). In France, Bourbon acted as tutor to Jeanne d'Albret, daughter of Margaret, Queen of Navarre, and mother of Henri IV.

(Parker 37; QG 18; RL 12192)

ANONYMOUS SIXTEENTH-CENTURY ARTIST after HOLBEIN: Nicholas Bourbon, 1535 (woodcut, from N. Bourbon, *Nugae*)

Nicholas Borbonius Poeta.

48

George Brooke, 9th Baron Cobham

Black and coloured chalks, pen and black ink, and some metalpoint, on pink prepared paper. 289 × 203 mm. Inscribed in tarnished gold over red: *Brooke L^dCobham*.

George Brooke was a member of an ancient noble family, and several of his relations sat to Holbein for their portraits. His sister was married to the poet Wyatt (No. 45), and in 1547 his daughter Elizabeth became the second wife of William Parr, Marquis of Northampton (No. 33). He was born c. 1497, the son of Thomas Brooke, 8th Baron Cobham, whom he succeeded in 1529. George Brooke was frequently at Court and had received a knighthood in 1523, after the capture of Morlaix. He was among those officiating at Anne Boleyn's trial in 1536, and was a strong supporter of the King's new religious policies. He was appointed Deputy of Calais in 1544 and served as Lieutenant General in the Scottish campaign of 1546. He was elected a Knight of the Garter in 1549, while serving in the French wars. During the reign of Queen Mary he was implicated in the younger Wyatt's rebellion, but was pardoned. He died in 1558.

Vertue noted a drawing of Lord Cobham by Holbein in the collection of Lady Elizabeth Germain (Vertue, *Notebooks*, V, p. 21). No painting connected to this drawing was known until Rowlands published a roundel (measuring 312 mm diameter), which passed through the London sale rooms in 1969 and is now in a private collection in West Germany (Rowlands, cat. no. R. 38). This portrait bears the following (contemporary?) inscription: GEORGIUS DOMINUS DE COBHAM GUBERNATOR CALETTI ET PATER GVLIHELLM. DE COBHAM. As Cobham was appointed to Calais only in the year after Holbein's death, this may provide additional evidence for an attribution of the painting to a follower of Holbein, evidently basing his work on this drawing.

The explanation for the somewhat informal costume depicted in No. 48 (which is slightly altered in the picture) is surely not merely that Holbein 'could only catch these busy courtiers at an odd moment, perhaps early in the morning, or returning from some form of exercise' (Rowlands, p. 236). The portraits of Cobham's brother-in-law Wyatt incorporate similarly casual dress. The black chalk shading of the side of the face is remarkable, and is reproduced in the painted roundel noted above. The drawing probably dates from the very end of Holbein's life, c. 1540/43.

(Parker 53; QG 66; RL 12195)

Brooke Ld Cobham.

49

SIMON GEORGE

Black and coloured chalks, and black ink applied with pen and brush, on pink prepared paper.   279 × 191 mm. Inscribed in gold over red, in a cursive hand: *S George of Cornwall*.   Watermark: type J (Briquet 1255)

The sitter has been identified as Simon George, who is recorded in the following words in the heraldic visitation of Cornwall in 1620: 'Simon George came to Quotoule in Com. Cornwall'. His father and grandfather came from Dorset and he was married to Thomasine, daughter of Richard Lanian of Cornwall, who died in 1587 and whose family originated in Gloucestershire (Rowlands, p. 144, and Foister, p. 42). There is no record of Simon George's presence at Court, and the circumstances in which he met Holbein are likewise unknown. The precise location of 'Quotoule' is also far from clear. No place of that name is now known. While it could be a variant of Cotehele, the modern spelling was already in use there in the sixteenth century.

This drawing has obvious affinities with Holbein's painted roundel of the same sitter in the Städelsches Institut, Frankfurt-am-Main (measuring 310 mm diameter; Rowlands, cat. no. 63). X-radiography of the Frankfurt panel has shown that in the under-drawing the sitter was depicted without the thick beard that he wears in the final painting. The delicacy in the treatment of detail in the painting, and the *trompe l'oeil* effect of the embroidered cuff folded back against the picture frame, make it a notable item in Holbein's *oeuvre*. The drawing has a somewhat unfinished feel to it, and the faint chalk indications of the jacket seem to show a different garment from the one finally painted. A date in the mid-1530s would seem likely for both drawing and painting.

(Parker 35; QG 39; RL 12208)

HANS HOLBEIN THE YOUNGER: Simon George (oil on panel; Frankfurt, Städelsches Institut)

S. George of Cornwall

50

AN UNIDENTIFIED LADY

Black and coloured chalks with white bodycolour and pen and black ink, on pink prepared paper. The drawing has been cut around the edges and mounted onto a fresh sheet of paper. 268 × 166 mm. Inscribed by the artist in pen and ink: *Samat* (velvet) and *damast* (damask). VERSO inscribed in ink and again in chalk: *hans holbein*. Watermark (on the drawn sheet): type E (variant of Briquet 12863)

The identity of this strikingly portrayed lady is not recorded, nor is a painted version of this image known. The rigid frontal stance might suggest a connection with the Howard family portraits (Nos 20, 21 and 23). The old identifications as Anne or Amelia of Cleves appear to be without foundation. The subtly modelled left side of the face, bordered by a stark black hairline, has something in common with Cardinal Fisher's haunting image (No. 10). The quality of the pen work is very fine, particularly in the eyes and eyebrows. Typically, the repeating pattern on the high collar of the shirt is sketched in detail only once, and the materials of the bodice are noted. This portrait was probably taken c. 1535.

At an unknown date this drawing became separated from the others in the 'great booke', and was cut around in silhouette, as were two other drawings now in the Louvre and in the British Museum. It bears the collector's mark of Jonathan Richardson the Elder (Lugt 2184) and later belonged to Dr Richard Mead. At Mead's sale in 1755 the drawing was acquired by Walter Chetwynd, whose heir (Benjamin Way, of Denham) was stated by Chamberlaine to have 'lately had the honour of receiving his Majesty's permission to add it to the Royal Collection' (J. Chamberlaine, *Imitations of Original Drawings by Hans Holbein* . . ., London, 1792–1800, vol. I, No. 3).

(Parker 47; QG 43; RL 12190)

Appendix: The Watermarks

A proper study of the different types of paper used in the Windsor Holbein series has been possible for less than ten years, following the remounting of the drawings between thin sheets of acrylic and the subsequent photography of the watermarks. It is not possible to study the drawings by Holbein in other collections in the same way. Although Ganz mentioned the watermark type in his pioneering catalogue (P. Ganz, *Les Dessins de Hans Holbein le jeune*, Geneva, 1939), his references are far from reliable. The following statements are therefore in no way conclusive, but may indicate possible future lines of enquiry.

The recent remounting of the Windsor Holbein drawings revealed fourteen different watermark types, of which twelve are represented in the drawings included in the present catalogue. (The omitted marks are a variant of Briquet 12691/841 found on Parker 74, and an unrecorded mark of a deer's head found on Parker 82.) Twenty-seven of the forty-nine catalogued drawings bear watermarks. Although all the drawings (with the possible exception of No. 12) were executed in England, the paper was in no case of English origin. Paper-making did not become properly established in England until around fifty years after Holbein's death, in spite of John Tate's abortive attempt to set up a mill near Hertford in the 1490s (see A. H. Shorter, *Paper Mills and Paper Makers in England*, 1495–1800, Hilversum, 1957: vol. VI of *Monumenta Chartae Papyraceae Historiam Illustrantia*, especially pages 27–28). In common with contemporary government officers and book printers, Holbein used paper imported from the Continent, and in particular from France and the Netherlands.

The following individual descriptions have been arranged according to type, rather than catalogue number. The types are given in the approximate order in which Holbein used them, rather than in the order of the first appearance of each watermark as given by Briquet. Thus chronologically the first watermark is Briquet 1457 (type D), which is recorded on documents in Utrecht in 1519–21, but was used by Holbein on drawings such as No. 35, of Sir Richard Southwell, which is directly related to a portrait of 1536. Briquet 12863 (first recorded in documents in The Hague in 1524) is our type A, as it appears in four of the More family drawings, datable c. 1526–28. (However, it reappears in No. 39, datable over ten years later.) It is indicative of the present regional basis of watermark studies that some of the drawings in this catalogue appear to bear watermarks not otherwise recorded until several years after the probable date of Holbein's usage. Thus Briquet 11369 (type H) is found on No. 20, the study of Mary, Duchess of Richmond and Somerset. Although the first recorded instance of this paper given in Briquet is Utrecht, 1541, Holbein's portrait of the Duchess is normally dated to early in his second English period, c. 1533.

The above statements bear out the general tenet that until watermark studies have advanced considerably beyond the formidable work of Briquet, few useful conclusions can be drawn. This is particularly the case so far as papers in use in England in the first half of the sixteenth century are concerned. For each watermark type, only one actual-size line drawing is given (traced from a catalogued drawing, the number of which is followed by an asterisk), on the grounds that every mark will have (sometimes scarcely perceptible) differences from the pattern given by Briquet. Where the distance between chain lines differs, variations are given. Locations and dates of other recorded instances of each mark, as given by Briquet, are copied selectively.

TYPE A
Two-handled vase with double flower cresting
Briquet 12863: The Hague, 1524; Brunswick, 1526. The two-handled vase type originated in the Champagne region of France.

Nos 1, 2, 6 and 8: for the More family group, c. 1526–28 (chain lines wider apart, 2.5 to 3 cm; 11-12 laid lines to the cm)
No. 17 (unidentified gentleman), c. 1533
No. 32 (James Butler, Earl of Ormond), c. 1535
No. 39* (William Fitzwilliam, Earl of Southampton), late 1530s
The same mark appears on Parker 9, 40 and 77.

TYPE B
Crowned shield containing three fleur-de-lys (the arms of France)
Briquet 1827: Châlons-sur-Marne, 1522; Amsterdam, 1523; Bruges, 1523

No. 3 (Sir Thomas More), 1527
No. 9 (Sir Henry Guildford), 1527
No. 11* (William Warham), 1527
The same mark appears on the portrait of Warham sold at Christie's, London, 4th July 1984 (lot 139)
The spacing of the chain lines is irregular and varies from 2.3 to 3.3 cms in any one sheet.

TYPE C
Hand topped by five-pointed star
Smaller variant of Briquet 11341/42: Lisieux, 1526; Rouen, 1527; Thury, 1527. The hand is a common mark in France throughout the sixteenth century.

No. 10* (John Fisher), c. 1532. The thick priming has obscured both laid and chain lines.

TYPE D
Crowned double-headed eagle, with tailpiece
Larger variant of Briquet 1457: Utrecht, 1519–21

No. 23 (Frances, Countess of Surrey), c. 1532: cropped above tailpiece
No. 35* (Sir Richard Southwell), 1536
The same mark appears (in part) on Parker 44 and 48, on Parker 68 and, in variant form, on the portrait of the lady formerly called Anne Boleyn, in the British Museum (1975-6-21-22).

TYPE E
Two-handled vase with single-flowered cresting
Not in Briquet, but close to type A (Briquet 12863, etc.), although smaller and lacking the upper flower.

No. 22* (Henry Howard, Earl of Surrey), c. 1532–35
No. 50 (unidentified lady), c. 1535
The same mark appears on Parker 20, 36 and 77.

TYPE F
Hand topped by crown
Close to Briquet 11391: Neubourg, 1535; Caen, 1540–41

No. 27* (Queen Anne Boleyn?), c. 1533–35
No. 44 (John Colet), c. 1532: variations in angle of thumb and shape of wrist

TYPE G
Crowned shield containing three fleur-de-lys with diagonal pattern, and initials VP (?) below
Variant of Briquet 1050 (type G lacks crowning flower): Brussels, 1530; Utrecht, 1533–42; Cleves, 1535–45. The arms identify this paper as from the mill of Fontaine près Bar-sur-Aube, near Troyes.

No. 13 (Margaret, Lady Elyot), c. 1532–34
No. 16 (Elizabeth, Lady Vaux), c. 1536
No. 43* (Sir Nicholas Poyntz), c. 1535

TYPE H
Hand with figure 3 in palm, topped by five-pointed star
Close to Briquet 11369: Utrecht, 1541; Bruges, 1545; Hamburg, 1546

No. 20* (Mary, Duchess of Richmond and Somerset), c. 1532
The same mark appears on Parker 54 (in which the hand is set between rather than upon the chain lines) and on Parker 65 (a copy of No. 45).

TYPE I
Lion holding orb and shield (the arms of Zurich)
Briquet 878: Zurich, 1536; Augsburg, 1542

No. 31* (Mary Zouche), c. 1532–36
The same mark appears on Parker 52, 78, 79 and 84. The latter drawing is not by Holbein.

TYPE J
Crowned shield topped by flower, containing cross and goose
Briquet 1255: Bruges, 1525–34; Troyes, 1532, 1535–39

No. 49* (Simon George), c. 1535

TYPE K
Hand with figure 3 in palm and initials RP across wrist, topped by five-pointed star
Briquet 11387: Hamburg, 1544 and 1550

No. 36* (Richard, Baron Rich), c. 1540
No. 37 (Elizabeth, Lady Rich), c. 1540

TYPE L
Gothic letter p with split tail
Briquet 8653 (omitting the flower): Rotterdam, 1532. The gothic 'P' appears on French papers from as early as 1445.

No. 29* (Sir Philip Hoby), c. 1539.
No. 30 (Elizabeth, Lady Hoby), c. 1539.
The mark on No. 30 is fragmentary. The same mark probably appears on Parker 62 (with the flower) and 70.

TYPE A

TYPE B

TYPE C

TYPE D

TYPE E

TYPE F

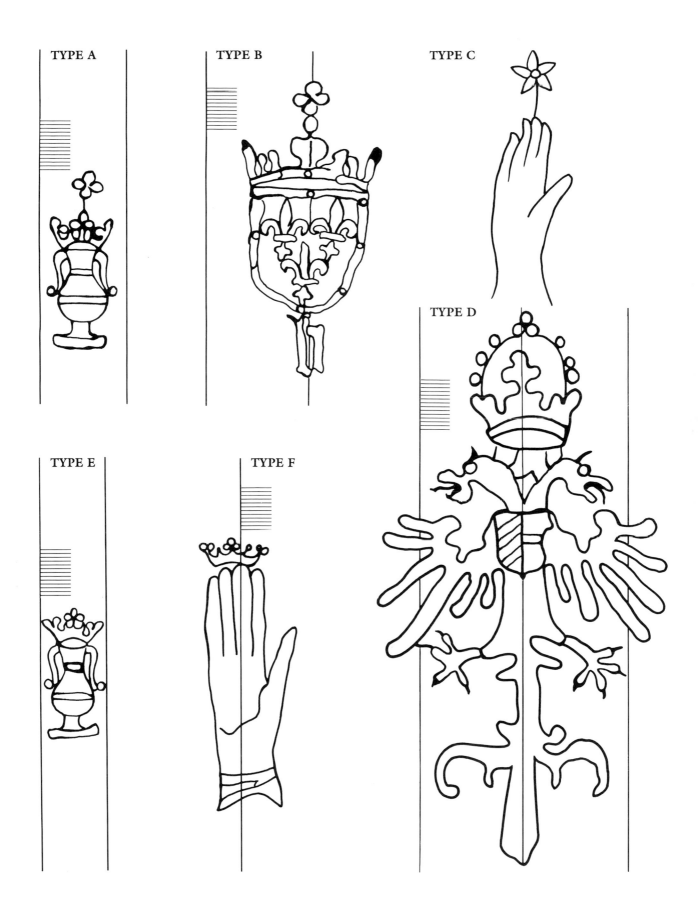

143

TYPE G

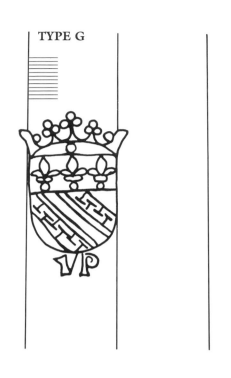

TYPE H

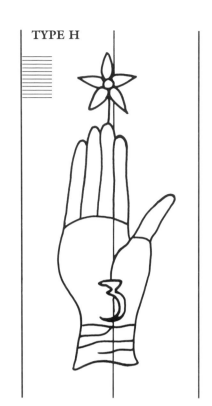

TYPE I

TYPE K

TYPE J

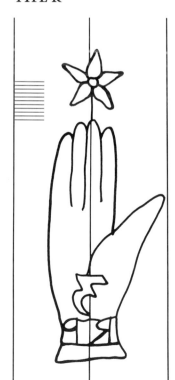

TYPE L

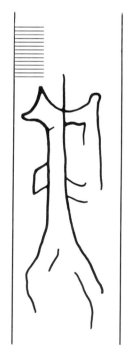

Works Referred to in Abbreviated Form

Briquet   C. M. Briquet, *Les Filigranes*, Paris, 1907; reprinted Amsterdam, 1968

Burl. Mag.   *The Burlington Magazine*

Foister   S. Foister, *Drawings by Holbein from the Royal Library, Windsor Castle*, New York, 1983 (the numbering in the catalogue follows that in Parker)

J.W.C.I.   *Journal of the Warburg and Courtauld Institutes*

Millar   O. Millar, *The Tudor, Stuart and Early Georgian Pictures in the Collection of H. M. The Queen*, London, 1963

Parker   K. T. Parker, *The Drawings of Hans Holbein in the Collection of His Majesty The King at Windsor Castle*, Oxford and London, 1945; reprinted, with an Appendix by Susan Foister, New York, 1983 (see also Foister)

Parthey   G. Parthey, *Wenzel Hollar*, Berlin, 1853; expanded by R. Pennington, *A Descriptive Catalogue of the Etched Work of Wenceslaus Hollar*, Cambridge, 1982

QG   *Holbein and the Court of Henry VIII*, exhibition catalogue, The Queen's Gallery, Buckingham Palace, London, 1978–79

Rowlands   J. Rowlands, *Holbein: The Paintings of Hans Holbein the Younger, Complete Edition*, Oxford, 1985

Strong   R. Strong, *National Portrait Gallery. Tudor and Jacobean Portraits*, 2 vols. London, 1969

Concordance of Drawings

Parker	Cat. No.	Parker	Cat. No.	Parker	Cat. No.
Frontispiece	24	18	23	51	30
1	1	22	38	53	48
2	2	23	32	55	37
3	3	24	15	57	33
4	5	25	16	58	40
5	7	29	22	59	44
6	4	31	19	61	42
7	6	32	17	63	27
8	8	33	18	64	45
10	9	34	43	66	39
11	12	35	49	67	34
12	11	37	47	69	41
13	10	38	35	72	31
14	13	39	26	73	28
15	14	46	25	76	46
16	20	47	50	80	36
17	21	50	29		

Index of Names

Numbers shown are those in the catalogue